FEAR NOT!

By Martha Smock

Compiled by Jeanne Allen

Unity Books
Unity Village, MO 64065

Cover photo by Margarite Hoefler

2/9/

Copyright © 1986 by Unity School of Christianity
Unity Village, MO 64065
Library of Congress Catalog Card 86-050434
ISBN 0-87159-037-9

Table of Contents

Fear Not!

The words *fear not* have a biblical sound, and well they might, for this phrase runs throughout the Bible. *Cruden's Complete Concordance* lists this phrase as appearing 79 times.

The Bible does not tell us that we shall never be without fear. But again and again we are given the assurance, "Fear not." In the Old and New Testaments, these words are spoken in dreams, in visions; they are spoken by angels, by prophets; they are spoken by Jesus. They are God's word to any who are afraid for any reason.

That this assurance is given so many times throughout the Bible tells us something about us and our relationship with God.

We may be prone to fear for one reason or another, but we do not need to succumb to it. We may have to work to overcome our fear, but always there is something in us that urges us not to give in to fear, that says, "Fear not."

Why do we fear? What do we fear?

Sometimes we think that we have overcome all fear, then something occurs, and without warning, and to our dismay, we feel fearful and apprehensive.

Perhaps it is a physical condition that causes us to be afraid.

Perhaps it is an unexpected change of circumstances that brings us face to face with unknown situations, with strange places, with people who are strangers, that makes us feel insecure and anxious.

Perhaps we are called on to do something for which we do not feel qualified or prepared, and we fear failure.

Perhaps our security is threatened, and we are fearful that we will not have supply for our needs.

Perhaps our fear is for another person. We

are alarmed over a dear one's state of health, or we are fearful for his safety, or a dear one does not arrive at an expected time and we begin to picture dire happenings.

If we have such feelings of fear, especially when we had thought that we had overcome fear, we can be thankful that these fears have surfaced, because we have the opportunity to reassert our faith and fearlessness and banish even the trace of fear.

No person has ever been completely without fear, but every person can learn to handle fear when it arises, can turn fear into faith, into courage, into positive thoughts and feelings and actions.

"Fear not" is an assurance needed not only by the weak or the wavering; it is an assurance needed by the brave, the strong, and the courageous.

We sometimes see a person who seems always to be in control of the situation, who never seems afraid, and we think that this person has never known fear. He has probably known fear, but has learned to handle it, to overcome it, to make the fearful occasion an occasion to prove the power of God, an occasion to let the power of God, the courage of God flow through him in strength and might.

Let's think about some of the "Fear nots" in the Bible. We are familiar with many of these assurances.

Are we afraid to be alone?

> *Fear not, for I am with you.*
> *For I, the Lord your God,*
> *hold your right hand;*
> *it is I who say to you, "Fear not,*
> *I will help you."*

(Isa. 41:10-13)

There are times in our lives when we find ourselves alone, when we must meet something alone. But we are never alone. God is with us. We have nothing to fear.

Are we fearful concerning our health?

> *Strengthen the weak hands,*
> *and make firm the feeble knees.*
> *Say to those who are of a fearful heart,*
> *"Be strong, fear not!"*

(Isa. 35:3, 4)

Whatever the condition, we have nothing to fear, for we live in the midst of God's life. God's healing power is mighty in the midst of us to heal every disease. God's healing, loving presence enfolds us.

Are we afraid of being unloved, unneeded?

"Fear not, therefore; you are of more value than many sparrows" (Matt. 10:31).

We are unique and wonderful children of God, beloved of God, needed and important to God and to God's world. Knowing this, we have no fear.

Are we afraid of being unworthy?

"Fear not, for you will not be ashamed" (Isa. 54:4).

Sometimes people carry with them thoughts of guilt and unworthiness and feel that they cannot be forgiven. But God sees us as worthy. God's loving forgiveness is poured out upon all. God's love says to anyone who feels unworthy, "Fear not, you are set free from the past. You can begin again."

Are we afraid of people?

"Fear not the reproach of men" (Isa. 51:7).

"Fear not, for am I in the place of God?" (Gen. 50:19)

We are not afraid of people when we remember that they, too, are children of God, when we behold the Christ in them as well as in ourselves. We feel in harmony with other people, and the love of God in our hearts casts out all fear.

Are we afraid to make a decision, to take some step that we feel is right?

"Be strong and of good courage, and do it. Fear not, be not dismayed; for the Lord God, even my God, is with you. He will not fail you or forsake you" (I Chron. 28:20).

We find it easy to make decisions, to act without fear or hesitation as we know that God is with us, that God's wisdom guides us, that God's light shines before us to make plain our way.

Are we afraid that our prayers have gone unanswered?

"Fear not; for God has heard" (Gen. 21:17).

"I will be with you, and will bless you" (Gen. 26:3).

We can release all our needs and problems lovingly into God's care, knowing that even before we pray, God's answer is there. We have nothing to fear, for God is our help in every need, the perfect answer to every prayer.

Are we afraid that we will be unjustly treated? Are we afraid of the outcome of some situation?

"Fear not, stand firm, and see the salvation of the Lord, which he will work for you today" (Exod. 14:13).

We have nothing to fear when we place our trust in God, when we stand firm in our faith in God's divine law of justice, when we know that all things are working out in right and perfect ways for us and for all concerned.

Are we afraid of lack?

"Fear not, little flock, for it is your Father's good pleasure to give you the kingdom" (Luke 12:32).

When we realize that God's abundance is poured out upon us, that there is no lack in God, no limit to God's provision for us, we have no fear. We know that our needs will be taken care of, that we will have plenty to spare and to share.

Whenever we are fearful for any reason, let us remind ourselves of these reassuring words, "Fear not."

We should not be discouraged if occasionally we have to work at not being afraid. We can look back and see how we have grown through such times. The times we were fearful but found the courage to face fear and overcome it—were not these times of spiritual growth, times for which we can be thankful?

Fear in itself has no power except the power we give it through our thoughts. We take away its power, we put it to rout, as we know that there is nothing to fear, that we are never alone, that always God is with us.

God within us says to us, "Fear not!"

"Fear not, I am the first and the last, and the living one" (Rev. 1:17, 18).

"Fear not, for I have redeemed you;
    I have called you by name, you are
        mine."

(Isa. 43:1)

Fear not!

Words, a Call to Courage

Sometimes one line or even one phrase spoken at the right moment becomes unforgettable. It acts as a rallying call to courage. On March 4, 1933, in the depths of the Depression, Franklin Delano Roosevelt, in his first Inaugural Address, said: *The only thing we have to fear is fear itself.* These words were a rallying call to courage, needed in that hour!

Think about the power of words, how they can be a rallying call to courage. For instance, the words, *God is my all, I know no fear* from "The Prayer of Faith" helped me to overcome childhood fears. These are words to turn to when courage is needed: *God is my all, I know*

no fear. A simple statement of faith—a rallying call to courage.

Lowell Fillmore once told about trying to
help a man who had come to him for counsel-
ing. Lowell said that no matter what he said,
the man just sat there, dejected, unrespon-
sive, fearful. Finally, almost in desperation,
Lowell said, "Well, you know, it's always
darkest before dawn." The man's eyes bright-
ened, he jumped up, shook Lowell's hand, and
exclaimed, "That's what I've been waiting to
hear!" What might have been a banal obser-
vation to some was his rallying call to
courage!

Affirmations of Truth are rallying calls to
courage. A Catholic nun confided that in the
eyes of the world she is an old, retired nun.
Her rallying call to courage is the affirmation: *I am the ever-renewing, ever-unfolding
expression of infinite life.* She says, "I feel
young, vital, growing."

It was a Sunday evening. I was at a young
people's meeting—an unhappy teenager, going through the throes of a broken romance.
We were singing a familiar hymn when I
heard, as though for the first time, the words:

Be not dismayed, whate'er betide,
God will take care of you.
They were my rallying call to courage. To
this day, when I hear this hymn and the
words *Be not dismayed, whate'er betide*, I
feel again the strength and renewal of spirit
that I experienced that long-ago Sunday evening.

The Bible is filled with rallying calls to
courage. The words: *"Be strong and of good*
courage, do not fear or be in dread of them: for
it is the Lord your God who goes with you; he
will not fail you or forsake you" (Deut. 31:6),
are a rallying call to courage. What is there to
fear? God is with you, whatever you do,
wherever you go. You are not alone, you are
never without help.

The story is told of a woman who was ac-
costed by two men as she walked alone on a
dark street. Her rallying call to courage in
that terrifying moment was from the 91st
Psalm. She said them in a loud voice. *"He*
covers me with his feathers! He covers me
with his feathers!" One of the men said to the
other, "She's crazy! Leave her alone."

As a child, I was afraid of dogs, especially

barking dogs. I don't know that I tried to conquer this fear. I did my best to avoid dogs, even to the extent of going blocks out of my way rather than meet up with one. One time as I was walking home, a dog appeared and began to bark. Suddenly there flashed into my mind the words, *perfect love casts out fear.* These words were a rallying call to courage for me, and I bravely proceeded on my way. The dog proved to be friendly. *Perfect love casts out fear.* This is true about any kind of fear—fear of dogs, fear of flying, fear of elevators and high places, fear of people. *There is no fear in love, but perfect love casts out fear* (I John 4:18)—a rallying call to courage! We need not be afraid. God's love is in our hearts, and love casts out fear. Love is stronger than fear, love is mightier than fear, love knows no fear.

The 23rd Psalm has been a rallying call to courage to people over the centuries. It is a rallying call to courage to us today when we need comfort and strength, when we meet loss or bereavement, when our way looks dark. God shows us green pastures. He leads us beside still waters; He restores our souls.

Though we walk through the valley of the shadow of death, there is nothing to fear. God is with us to uphold and comfort us. God's goodness and mercy shall be with us all the days of our lives and throughout eternity.

Charles Fillmore's words: *No one ever went down to defeat who in his hour of need declared the almightiness of God in Christ* were a rallying call to courage to me when I was faced with a serious health challenge. These words helped me to take heart, they helped me to overcome fear, to determine to prove the power of God to heal. They did not say "healing," but they were what I needed to hear at that time to help me to make my stand for health.

A woman who was ill and weak and lacking in strength found the Bible verse: *Let the weak say, I am strong* (Joel 3:10, A.V.). It was her rallying call to courage. She began affirming, *I am strong, I am strong,* and eventually regained her strength and health. She became a Unity minister and served for many years.

"With God all things are possible" (Matt. 19:26), a rallying call to courage when appear-

ances are alarming, when it seems that some condition is hopeless or incurable! *"With God all things are possible."* These words embolden us to say, "I will not fear. I will have faith. I will believe. I will hold fast to the Truth. Nothing is beyond God's power to heal."

God did not give us a spirit of timidity but a spirit of power and love and self-control. These words can be a rallying call to courage when we hang back in fear, when we are upset and anxious, when we are timid and fearful of persons and situations, when we are filled with self-doubt. God did not give us a spirit of timidity but of power and love and self-control. God has given us a powerful and loving spirit; God has given us the ability to control our thoughts and feelings. God has given us the faith and the will to succeed.

I read a little verse that acted as a rallying call to courage to me when I needed more faith—more faith in myself, more faith in my ability to accomplish the work that was mine to do. I have shared this verse, or prayer, which it really is, by Florence Taylor, with others who have also found it to be a faithincreaser, a spirit-booster.

> I thank Thee, Father, for the way
> Thy hand has guided me today.
> I woke at morning's dawn afraid
> To face my problems. But I prayed,
> And one by one each need was met;
> For Thou hast never failed me yet.
> Dear God, henceforth my prayer shall be
> For strong, abiding faith in Thee.

If there is something you want to do and ought to do but fear to do, do that thing and the very doing of it will set you free. These words seemed to leap off the page at me at a time when I was hesitant and fearful. They were a rallying call to courage. Do the thing you fear to do but know you ought to do, and the doing of it will set you free. The way to be free from fear is to act in faith. Fear can have its good side if it impels us to act, if it arouses a spirit of courage in us, if it dares us to face it. The rallying call to courage is always sounding, urging us to brush fear aside and to act decisively and fearlessly.

When the world seemed to be in chaos, engulfed in darkness during World War II, the following lines by an English poet, M. Louise

Haskins, were a rallying call to courage for many:

And I said to the man who stood at the gate of the year: "Give me a light that I may tread safely into the unknown."

And he replied:

"Go out into the darkness and put your hand into the Hand of God. That shall be to you better than a light and safer than a known way."

So I went forth and finding the Hand of God, trod gladly into the night. And He led me toward the hills and the breaking of day in the lone East.

All of us have times when we cannot see our way, when we have to go out into the darkness on faith. But finding the hand of God, or, in other words, feeling God's presence with us, we are guided safely and surely out of darkness into light. Our faith in God is "better than a light and safer than a known way."

Your Words Can Change Your World

Once I was in a department store waiting to have the salesclerk ring up my purchase. A woman walked up to the desk and the clerk asked, "How are you?" The woman answered, "Fine," and then said, "No, not really!" She proceeded to elaborate on all the things wrong with her. I am sure she was not aware of the negative effect this was having on her, on the way she felt about herself.

There is a little song that lifts me up on those days when all is right with the world, but especially on those days when I may not feel as strong, as vital, as joyous about life as I know I should:

I feel wonderful, I feel wonderful,

for this is a glorious day!
I feel wonderful, I feel wonderful,
and I am going to stay that way!

These words are like a little prayer, a little affirmation of life and well-being, and singing them to myself, repeating them to myself, has changed the day for me, has lifted me out of feelings of lack.

Our bodies respond to our thoughts and feelings, to our words. The cells of our bodies are listening, are ready to respond to words of faith and joy and life.

Affirmations of Truth are powerful reminders to us of the great potential in us for joyous, healthy, successful living. These affirmations become life-giving words to us as we meditate on them and let their truth sink deep into our consciousness. These affirmations set the tone, underlie our response to life. They focus our attention on God and all that God is. They align us with God; they center us in spiritual reality.

When it appears that we are not expressing the perfect health that God means for us, or when someone near and dear to us is in need of healing, we have wonderful words of life to lift us up, to hasten healing. Healing assurances are found throughout the Bible. *"I will come and heal him"* (Matt. 8:7).

"Then shall your light break forth like the dawn, and your healing shall spring up speedily" (Isa. 58:8).

Your faith has made you well.

As you hold fast in faith, as you pray, wonderful words of life will be revealed to you. You will feel God's loving presence within you, you will hear the still small voice saying, "I am your life. Be healed. Be free."

In the midst of lack, inflation, recession, difficult times, we can counteract fearful thinking with words that proclaim and affirm God as the unfailing source, the unfailing supply of all our needs. Outer conditions do not, cannot, limit God. Appearances do not discourage us as we keep our inner faith and conviction strong, as we affirm wonderful words of life-giving substance, as we know that God opens ways where there seems to be no way, that God prospers and guides and leads us into success.

The belief in age as a deterrent to happy, healthy living is a subtle one that we do not want to allow to take hold in our consciousness. One time I was selecting a birthday card and a woman standing next to me said, "I'm looking for a card for that terrible age." I said, "Oh, what age is that?" She said, "Thirty!" She went on to tell me that on her son's fortieth birthday, she baked him a birthday cake and iced it in black! It was all in a spirit of fun, I'm sure, but too many of us start thinking in terms of being old almost before we have begun to live.

Certainly, we need not and should not think in terms of old age at thirty or forty or at any age, for that matter. All of us want to be going forward, learning and growing, we want to be in the stream of life, and we should be, we can be. Years have nothing to do with it.

We are right now in the midst of eternal life. We are ageless, deathless, free Spirit. If we find ourselves falling in line with the belief that we are too old to accomplish the things we want to accomplish, too old to be really well and strong, let us recharge our thinking with wonderful words of eternal life such as "I am the resurrection and the life," or "I am the ever-renewing, ever-unfolding expression of infinite life." An idea that has been of help to me in rising above the belief in age as limiting is, "I am neither old nor young. I am Spirit."

Words play an important part in our human relationships. Some words are better left unsaid; words spoken thoughtlessly, words spoken defensively because we feel hurt or rejected, words we wish we could recall. But loving words are always welcome; they are words that everyone likes to hear, words that are never regretted.

Sometimes we need to speak loving words to ourselves. We may reject ourselves, we may have a poor self-image, we may be unforgiving of ourselves, we may feel unloved. The words *God loves me* can be wonderful words of life to us. To know that we are loved and that we have the capacity to express love can change our entire outlook on life.

We are constantly speaking all kinds of words, thinking all kinds of words. Why not make them wonderful words of life! Then we shall feel wonderful, and we shall stay that way!

Make a Positive Statement

Once when I was taking a class in oil painting, the teacher said to me and to others in
the class, "Make a positive statement!"

I have thought about this many times
since. Make a positive statement! Is not this
important in anything we do, from painting a
picture to baking a cake, to driving a car, to
living a life?

We make our lives positive statements as
we are not afraid to be ourselves, as we dare
to believe in God and in the good, as we color
our lives beautiful, as we develop bold, free,
unclouded outlooks and insights. We have a
vision of life that God has given us and we
need to hold to this vision, even if it means

beginning again and again, if the true picture does not at first emerge.

Make a positive statement! Is not this what we are doing every time we make an affirmation of Truth?

To make a positive statement in painting a picture, a person first of all must have a clear idea of what he is trying to paint. And he must have the right brushes, the right paints, and the know-how in using them.

Affirmations are a way of making a positive statement. Affirmations, the words themselves, are like the right brushes and the right paints necessary to create a picture. But, just as brushes and paints do not make a real painting, so the words of an affirmation in themselves are not enough. How we speak our affirmations—out of what faith, out of what understanding, out of what belief— makes the impact on us and on our lives.

Like the beginning artist, we do not have to know all about Truth, all about faith, all about God in order to start, in order to make a positive statement—right where we are, at our level of faith and understanding is the place to start.

The exciting thing is that when we begin even tentatively to affirm Truth, we tune in to the power of God within us. We hear a re-sounding "Amen" in the depths of us to the Truth when we affirm it, for the Spirit in us recognizes spiritual things and knows the Truth when it hears it.

Affirmations of Truth are power words; they are words that proclaim that which is real and eternal and unchanging. They say to us: "This is the truth about you! Believe it!"

Affirmations of Truth say to us: "Expect a miracle!" Faith in us answers, "Why not!"

Affirmations of Truth do not say, "This is true, if . . ." or "This is true, but . . ." They say to us: "This is the Truth. Hold to it, be-lieve it, make a positive statement with it!"

One might think that a person picking up *Daily Word* for the first time and reading the affirmations would reject them as far-fetched, perhaps even downright silly. It would not be surprising if this were the com-mon reaction, but such is not the case.

We hear from persons all the time who tell us that in their need someone handed them a *Daily Word,* or they picked it up somewhere, or someone sent them a gift subscription, and they found in it just the right word to help them, just the assurance they needed to give them faith and a new spirit.

One friend said that a few years ago *Daily Word* carried a very challenging affirmation: *I invite the loving power of God into my life.* He said that the lesson warned that this was a very powerful prayer and in using it to be prepared for results.

The winter following was an extremely difficult one, and he found himself fortifying himself against depression by repeating the affirmation. *I invite the loving power of God into my life.* He said that the affirmation was powerful and changes did come! He had turned depression into a positive statement.

What is the power of an affirmation of Truth? Why do we hold to it rather than reject it? It is because it puts into words that which we feel innately within us. Something in us recognizes the truth when we hear it; something in us responds to the idea that we are children of God, spiritual beings, able to do and be all that we long to do and be.

Begging, pleading prayer, prayers that are

self-accusatory, prayers that are steeped with guilt feelings, may perhaps ease a nagging conscience. However, they do not often bring a feeling of uplift. They may increase a feeling of separation from God. Such prayers are, of course, better than no prayers; in such prayers a person can, if he is sincere in seeking God's help and God's answer, finally feel an upliftment, make a breakthrough in his feeling of separation from God. If this occurs, his prayer becomes an affirmation, after all.

If a person feels weak and sick and prays: "O God, I feel weak and sick. I ask Your help. I beg Your forgiveness for all my many sins," he would certainly feel God's love and compassion. But he would probably not feel vital and alive. He needs to pray with faith, to make his prayer a positive statement. He needs to affirm his oneness with God and to know that God is life—the very life within him.

For instance, when we affirm: *I am alive with the life of Spirit and my body radiates health and wholeness,* we are stating that which is inherently true about us.

We are alive with the life of Spirit. The life

in us is God-life. We are created for life and
health and perfection. We do not need to beg
God for healing, for God is life and we are one
with that life.

What about making positive statements
for others?

Once I was scheduled to give a talk and I
said to my husband, "Pray for me." He answered: "I won't pray for you. I'll just know
that you will give a good talk." I said,
"That's what I mean by 'pray for me.' "

When we ask someone to pray for us, we do
not want him to be worried or anxious about
us. We may not even realize what it is we are
asking when we say, "Pray for me"; but what
we are really saying is, "Behold the good in
me. See God's power in me. Hold to the truth
with me. Have faith in me."

When we pray for others, let us be sure that
we are making positive statements about
them. This is the highest kind of prayer we
can make for another—to see him as God sees
him, to know that he is a spiritual being, to
have faith in the divine self of him.

We make our lives a positive statement
thought by thought, attitude by attitude,

prayer by prayer. It is a continuing process.

Recently a friend wrote to us, saying that she reads *Daily Word* every day. She asked, "Will I feel the power of God flowing through me if I keep reading? I want to believe what you say is true."

This question reminded us of another friend who told us that for many years she had begun each day with the page in *Daily Word*. She said that for a time she could not see that life was very different from what it would have been without *Daily Word.* "But now," she said, "it plays back to me, truly a path from the past into the future, and a bridge has been built over which I can walk." She has come to realize that she walks joyfully in spite of problems, because God walks with her, dwells within her, and life is very wonderful. Her day by day affirmation of Truth has made her life into a positive statement indeed!

How we pray a prayer determines whether it becomes a positive statement.

For instance, *Thy will be done* can be an affirmation, or it can be a prayer of resignation, even of fear. One man told us that all his life he had repeated these words, "Thy will be done," but like so many others he feared that God's will might not be the way he hoped and prayed things would work out. He said he finally reached a point of confusion where he did not know for sure what he wanted in the way of a solution. Then it came to him clearly that God's will could be only good. "Thy will be done" then became an affirmation of faith—faith in God, faith in the good. His life has since become a positive statement.

Charles Fillmore says: *Instead of a supplication, prayer should be a jubilant thanksgiving. This method of prayer quickens the mind miraculously, and, like a mighty magnet, draws out the spiritual qualities that transform the whole man when they are given expression in mind, body, and affairs.*

Make a positive statement! Make your prayers jubilant affirmations of Truth and life and power.

Expect a miracle! Why not?

No Other Way

"No Other Way" is the title of a poem I wrote years ago. Most writers are remembered for one piece of writing. I was thinking about this once when we sang "Irradiance" in Silent Unity. The beautiful words to this song were written by Ernest C. Wilson, and perhaps are better known and more loved and will be remembered longer than anything else he has written. James Dillet Freeman, who has written reams of poems, will perhaps be remembered for "I Am There." When we think of Frank B. Whitney, the first editor of *Daily Word,* we think of "I Behold the Christ in You." Maybe my best piece of writing is "No Other Way." Since it first appeared in

Daily Word in December 1947 I have heard from countless people about it. It seems to say something to them as it did to me when the words came through me.

Most of us, whether we realize it or not, have a recurring theme, an idea that we express again and again, in varying ways and words and acts. It is our theme song, as it were. No other way, the idea behind the words of this poem seems to have been my theme song.

In 1946 I wrote an article that preceded "No Other Way," but it really said the same thing. It was called, "The Stream of Life." In it I said that if we were to stand on a high hill and view a stream in the valley below, we should see all its twists and turns, its variation in width and depth, its troubled waters and turbulence; but from this high view we should see it as a whole. We should see how all was part of the flowing stream, ever going forward.

Should we be able to view our lives from a high hill in consciousness, we should see that they are not unlike a stream. Should we see with eyes free from a curtain of past or future, how days and months and years flow together, how all is swept along in the ceaseless progress of the soul, we should see that all of life is part of a whole. Though there be breaks and eddies and windings and turnings, still our lives flow ceaselessly and eternally, still our lives have purpose and wholeness. The mistakes of yesterday, the fears of yesterday, are as nothing in the ceaseless flow of life. We are learning and growing, following a pattern that we may not presently see, but that is emerging.

There are no isolated incidents in life though there may seem to be. No experience comes to us that is completely foreign to our consciousness, that has no relation to what we are. The happening that seems so tragic now, that seems to change our whole life, cannot and does not affect the ceaseless flow of life, does not stand unrelated to the past or future, but flows from the past and is absorbed into the future.

Can you remember the worries or fears of last year? Are they still as fearsome, as important as they were then? Next year, the year after, and the year after, will you even be able to remember them? And today's fear, which keeps your mind from rest and peace— will it be different from the rest? It will not. It too will pass. The stream of life flows on. "I'll never be happy again. I'll never love again," we say, but almost before the echo of our words has died away we have turned our hearts toward the new.

What we are today is the result of all that has gone before. One thing is certain, no matter what the experiences of our lives may be, we would not change places with anyone. We are unique creations. Something in us has always recognized the Truth. Something in us has always heard the inner voice which tells us that we are beloved of God, that we are expressions of the Christ.

We would not exchange our experiences for those of anyone else in the world, troubled though our stream of life may have been and rough our voyage. We would not be the unique individuals that we are without our particular background, without having passed through the experiences that life has brought to us, without having made the mental, emotional, and spiritual growth that we have made through the years. In the honesty of our hearts we must admit that we would not want to be anyone else, even if we could be. What we really want to be is the best possible self that we are capable of being.

No other way. Some years ago, I was facing a serious health challenge. May Rowland, a living example of Truth, wrote to me, "Just remember your poem, 'No Other Way.' " I remember thinking at the time, "I wish I had called it 'Some Other Way'!" But not really, for even out of what seem hard or difficult experiences we find our way and we gain and grow. May reminded me that we have the Unity work because Myrtle and Charles Fillmore needed healing. She said, "You, too, will have something to give because of this experience." I feel that this is true, that I have more understanding of what healing really is and that I am able to be more compassionate and helpful because of my experience.

If we can think of life as a flowing stream we come to learn that there are no failures, only the flowing of one experience into another. Have we failed to grasp some opportunity offered us? It is not the last opportunity that will ever be offered, and the fact that we did not grasp it indicates that we were not yet ready for it. But we shall be ready, and when we are, nothing can keep us from easily claiming and accepting our good.

Our lives are flowing in the direction of our good. Day by day we learn from the experiences that are part of our lives. We come to understand ourselves and to learn that we are an important part of humanity, and we shall draw to ourselves the experiences that are for our blessing; we shall find ourselves with the persons and in the places that are most conducive to our individual happiness.

When we look backward, we see how we have grown, how far we have come, but it is always a beginning, a time of rededication, a time of looking forward, of pressing forward, of setting new goals.

The wonderful teachings of Unity give us a true picture of ourselves, a picture of ourselves as eternal beings on an eternal journey. The teachings of Unity, the teachings of Jesus Christ help us to find meaning in everything, help us to find joy in day-to-day living, help us to fulfill the dreams we dream, to express the highest and best in us, to live up to our divine potential as spiritual beings.

The acronym for *no other way* is *now*. This, too, is what no other way means, that there is no other way to meet life than to meet it now, that now is the time to know the truth, now is the time to declare our freedom. Now is the time to live life fully, happily, healthily, successfully. Now is the time to know that we are beloved of God, that we are learning, growing, unfolding, and that life gets better, more beautiful, more delightful day by day.

You are a unique and wonderful creation. Your life has a pattern of good. Everything in your life, every step, every experience is a part of this pattern of growth and good. You are a living soul on an immortal, eternal journey, and the joy of journeying is to be found along the way, in the side trips and detours as well as in the ultimate destination.

No Other Way

Could we but see the pattern of our days,
We should discern how devious were the
     ways
By which we came to this, the present
     time,
This place in life; and we should see the
     climb
Our soul has made up through the years.
We should forget the hurts, the
     wanderings, the fears,
The wastelands of our life, and know
That we could come no other way or grow
Into our good without these steps our
     feet
Found hard to take, our faith found hard
     to meet.
The road of life winds on, and we like
     travelers go
From turn to turn until we come to know
The truth that life is endless and that we
Forever are inhabitants of all eternity.

Love Casts Out Fear

I believe that fear is conquered at all times and in all situations through love. *Perfect love casts out fear.* We cannot fear that which we love. Love casts out fear and frees us from bondage to it.

If you are afraid of something or someone, turn your thought and attention to what you love rather than dwell on the thought of fear. The following meditations can help you to cast out every thought of fear:

Love casts out fear of disease or ill health.

I love the life idea. I am in love with life. I think life, talk life. I see myself filled with life, the very life of God.

I love my body as a temple of the Holy

Spirit within me.

I love and praise and give thanks for the life of God that is my life, the life of God that heals and restores and makes new.

With thoughts and feelings of love—love of life, love of the healing idea—I cast out thoughts of ill health, of disease, of fear. I am in love with life, and I express the life of God radiantly, wonderfully, powerfully.

Love casts out fear of being alone.

I love my life. I love the place that I call my home. I love knowing that I am never alone, that always God is with me. I pour out my love and I feel surrounded and enfolded by the love of God.

I may be alone but I am never lonely. I think with love of dear ones near and far. I pray with love for the blessing of my dear ones and the blessing of the world. I feel a part of the great and wonderful family of God. Love makes me one with God and one with all God's children.

Love casts out fear of lack.

Love casts out poverty thoughts. I love the realization that I am a rich child of a rich Father. I love the work that is mine to do. I love and praise God as my dependable, unfailing resource. I love the flow of good that is endless. I love the supply that is without limitation. I love and use and express the talents and abilities with which I have been endowed. I love the feeling of success and satisfaction that I have because my trust is in God. I love the thought that my daily needs are met and that future needs will be met as well.

I express love and cast out thoughts of lack. I express love, prospering love, as I let myself be a channel of giving and receiving, as I share willingly and freely with others.

Love casts out fear of failure.

I love the opportunities that are set before me. I love the challenges that stir me to deeper thought, to greater effort. I love the spirit of faith and courage that rises up in me, that refuses to let fear dominate me.

I love the feeling of spiritual power that is mine when I act courageously, when I dare to step out on faith.

I love the feeling of reassurance that comes when I listen to my indwelling Christ telling me that I can succeed.

Love casts out fear of people.

Love, divine love, is never mistrusted, never mistrusts. Love, divine love, never mistreats, is never mistreated. Love is always harmonious. Love breaks down barriers of timidity or lack of understanding. Love is not overpowered by personality. Love meets in agreement with the best in others. Love reveals the good in others. Love sees the Christ in others.

I meet life and people in a loving spirit, and life and people respond to me with warmth and friendliness and love.

Love casts out fear of change.

I think about change that is taking place or may take place and I affirm: *I love the thought of change!* Love assures me that through every change God is with me, that in every changing condition or circumstance something new and rewarding, something that is of value and is a blessing is being revealed. I meet change with love and I am blessed by change, enriched by change, made happier by change.

Love casts out fear of fear.

Unreasoning fear, fear of I know not what—love casts out fear of fear itself! I remember that God loves me. What is there to fear? God is love and God loves me. Fear cannot stand in the face of love.

Neither death, nor life ... nor things present, nor things to come, nor powers, nor height, nor depth, nor anything else in all creation, will be able to separate us from the love of God (Rom. 8:38-39).

Fearlessly I meet life, loving God, knowing that God loves me and that nothing or no one can separate me from the love of God.

There is no fear in love, but perfect love casts out fear.

The Voice We Might Not Hear

We listen to many voices, voices that dwell on negative conditions, that predict all sorts of dire things, voices that would negate optimism and faith.

Perhaps someone pours out a tale of woe; perhaps we turn on the television and all the news seems bad; perhaps we read the headlines in the newspapers and wonder what the world is coming to.

The voice we sometimes do not hear is the inner voice, the voice of the Christ.

"In the world you have tribulation; but be of good cheer, I have overcome the world" (John 16:33). Not I will, I *have*. Christ in you has overcome the world. Listen to His voice.

When your life is upset, turned around by change—loss of a loved one, a broken romance, loss of a job, any of the circumstances of life that seem threatening to your peace of mind, to your very existence—listen to the voice of Christ saying: *"Let not your hearts be troubled, neither let them be afraid"* (John 14:27). *"Lo, I am with you always"* (Matt. 28:20).

Christ is your center, your anchor, your unchanging life. Christ in you says: "I am with you, unchanging, eternal. I am your center of peace. I am your anchor of stability. I am that in you which is strong and steadfast. I am the overcoming power in you. I show you the path of life. I am the way, the Truth, and the life. You can meet changing conditions and circumstances; you can rise up with courage and faith; you can go forward with confidence and joy. In me you can do all things."

In time of sadness or grief, listen to the Christ. *"Believe in God, believe also in me"* (John 14:1). *"Peace I leave with you; my peace I give to you; not as the world gives do I give to you"* (John 14:27).

Turn to the loving Christ and hear Christ

say, "Peace! Be still!" to the surging waves of emotion that would overpower you. In Christ you are calmed and quieted, you rest in Christ's presence and feel strengthened and upheld. Remember that though things change, God is changeless, enduring. God's love is eternal. God's life is eternal. You can never lose your own. You are always and forever one in Spirit with those whom you love. If your life seems to be going through an upheaval of change, Christ is at the heart of you, at the heart of all.

When you are depressed or down in spirit, when you feel unworthy, inferior, when you tell yourself that you do not have what it takes to succeed in life, there is something you sense but may not hear because you do not want to hear. But strong and persistent the voice is speaking. Something in you knows and has always known that there is yet more in you. You are dissatisfied and discouraged not because of what you lack but because of what you have not yet expressed.

There is yet more in you. Do you know how remarkable you are? Do you know that you are so much more than you believe yourself to be, that however small or great your accomplishments, there is yet more in you to be expressed? If you have thought of yourself as an ordinary person, if you feel that your efforts have not counted for much, I would remind you that you are not an ordinary person. You are a spiritual being. As a spiritual being you have divine potential; you have the capacity to add to the joy and gladness of life; you have the capacity to express love to others and to relate to others in love and understanding. You are an important part of life, and you are needed where you are.

Do not hold back in fear. Do not listen to the doubts and arguments of the limited personal self. Do not listen to the voice of pessimism. Do not listen to those who would discourage you. Listen to the inner voice which always assures you that you can do more, be more, express more, that you are meant for joyous, radiant, successful living.

Listen to the Christ who says: *"Do not judge by appearances, but judge with right judgment"* (John 7:24). Appearances can be frightening; appearances can seem overwhelming. But appearances are just that—

appearances. They are not Truth, they are not the reality of God.

If you are not to judge by appearances, what are you to judge by? You are to keep the high watch, to see beyond the appearance to the ultimate good. Every time you affirm Truth you are denying belief in appearances, you are placing your faith where it belongs—in God, in the Truth of God.

The appearance may be ill health, or disease. The truth is that life and healing are God's will, that you are meant to be well and whole and vitally alive. The truth is that your body is the temple of the living God, that the perfect body idea is always present, always comes forth as you affirm life.

Listen to the song of life within you. Every cell, every atom joins in the glorious symphony.

Listen to the Christ saying: *"I came that they may have life, and have it abundantly"* (John 10:10). I came that *you* may have life and have it abundantly. *"I am the resurrection and the life"* (John 11:25). I am the life-giving Spirit within you.

Listen to the word of life that vibrates

throughout your being. Speak words of life, enter the life stream, the eternal flow of life.

Is there the appearance of lack, lack of money, lack of work, lack of opportunity? *"Do not judge by appearances, but judge with right judgment"* (John 7:24). Keep the high watch of Truth. Look beyond appearances to the truth that God is the source of all supply and that there is no lack in God. You live in a rich world; you have a rich Father. You are always one with your source. The link between you and God is mind. The flow of good comes through you in the form of ideas. Prosperity begins in the inner realization of oneness with God, oneness with all good.

Have you been looking to outer things for supply, to places and persons? There are channels to be sure, but God is the source, and the source is within you.

"Do not be anxious about your life, what you shall eat, nor about your body, what you shall put on. For life is more than food, and the body more than clothing . . . Instead, seek his kingdom, and these things shall be yours as well" (Luke 12:22, 23, 31).

The kingdom of God is in the midst of you. Listen to the voice of Christ saying: *"Come, O blessed of my Father, inherit the kingdom prepared for you from the foundation of the world"* (Matt. 25:34). *"It is your Father's good pleasure to give you the kingdom"* (Luke 12:32). You have the assurance, as you listen in prayer and silence, that your every need can be met, is already met in Spirit. Through Christ in you, you can do all things. Through Christ in you, you can succeed and prosper.

Listen to the voice of love and forgiveness. *"Forgive, and you will be forgiven"* (Luke 6:37).

When voices from other days, voices from the past, rise up to remind you of old hurts, resentments, old mistakes, you are not overpowered by them as you listen to the voice of the Christ within you saying, "You are forgiven as you forgive. Forgive the debts of the past. Remember them no more."

Listen to the truth. The truth is that you are free from the bondage of the past. You are forgiven the mistakes of the past. The truth is that you can begin again.

"You will know the truth, and the truth will make you free" (John 8:32). Go your way with joy, free from the burden of guilt, free from self-condemnation, free to fulfill your divine potential, to be all that you can be, all that you were meant to be.

When you are anxious and worried about others, when the needs of dear ones seem great, when there seems little you can do, listen to the loving Christ. *"I in them and thou in me, that they may become perfectly one"* (John 17:23). The Christ in you beholds the Christ in others; beholding the Christ, you know that there is no need too great, no problem too complicated, no condition incurable or impossible. The Christ in you reminds you that with God all things are possible.

Are you going through a time of darkness? Listen to words of light:

"I have come as light into the world, that whoever believes in me may not remain in darkness" (John 12:46).

"I am the light of the world; he who follows me will not walk in darkness, but will have the light of life" (John 8:12).

"You are the light of the world" (Matt.

5:14). Let your light shine!

The light of Christ is your light. This light shines in your mind as intelligence and wisdom. Depression, darkness of thought or outlook, is banished in the pure shining of the Christ light. Your body, which seems to be mass and material, is composed of light. As you awaken to the Christ life within you, it is as though every cell lights up. Light and healing go hand in hand.

The light of Christ shines in you, it shines for you, it shines through you to bless the world. *"Let your light so shine before men, that they may see your good works and give glory to your Father who is in heaven"* (Matt. 5:16). Not to the personal self but to the Christ self is glory given. Your purpose is to live the truth, express the truth, show forth the truth.

Do you feel bound and limited by some circumstance or condition, by some person? Do you feel bound by some habit that you know you should release?

"You will know the truth, and the truth will make you free" (John 8:32). You will know the truth. What truth? The truth that you are a

spiritual being, that you have a spark of divinity in you, that you do not have to stay in bondage to any circumstance, to any condition. You will know the truth that you are not at the mercy of your moods, that you are not limited by past mistakes or failures, that you are the Christ of God in expression.

Restlessness of spirit, feelings of dissatisfaction, are overcome as you let Christ be lifted up in you. Christ is the way of freedom. *"If the Son makes you free, you will be free indeed"* (John 8:36). Your soul satisfaction comes from deep wells of peace within you. The living water of Spirit quenches your thirst; the living bread of Spirit satisfies your every hunger.

Listen to the voice of Christ that says: *"You did not choose me, but I chose you"* (John 15:16).

Do you think that you are unimportant, unneeded? You are here by divine appointment. You are an important part of God's plan, of God's creation. You have your unique role to fill.

What have you been chosen to do? You have been chosen to give expression to God, to the Christ qualities. You have been chosen to express love. You have been chosen to be a part of the flow of life. You have been chosen to contribute to the good, the happiness, the well-being of the world. You have been chosen to express your particular abilities and talents. You have been chosen to be a light in the world.

Its Name Is Practice

Two little girls were trying hard to master the technique of ballet. They awkwardly but persistently worked to get their feet in the proper positions—fifth position, second position, balance, twirl, and so on. But when the teacher told them she was going to give them a few calisthenics along with the ballet instruction and then said, "Let's see you do a cartwheel," it was as formidable a request as if she had said, "Let's see you jump over the moon!" Their attempts were ridiculous, but no one laughed. The only encouragement the teacher offered was, "Girls, you will just have to practice."

They did practice, but it was like practicing

the impossible, it seemed. Their attempts, and they were strenuous ones, did not produce cartwheels. Because they could see no results, they began to resist even the thought of cartwheels and made every excuse not to practice doing them.

One day they were riding in the backseat of a car, and the older one, a nine-year-old, picked up a *Unity* magazine that was lying on the seat and began to read to the seven-year-old. This is the paragraph she read in an astonished voice: *There is a teaching, a principle, higher and more powerful than the printed words of Truth. It is the higher teaching that makes a reality of the theory you have read. It is available to you, here and now. Its name is practice.*

"Stephanie!" she cried. "It means our cartwheels!"

The day came when the teacher said: "Very good, girls. I know that you have been practicing."

"Its name is practice." How simple, yet how profound a statement!

We all need to remember that there is no other way to perfect any skill than to practice. Like the little girls who performed the "miracle" of cartwheels, anyone who practices Truth principles will perform "miracles" in his or her own life. God, the great Teacher, says, "Here is the way." Then it is up to us to try, again and again, to raise the level of our consciousness to the place where we cannot only know Truth but live it, express it.

There is a teaching, a principle, higher and more powerful than the printed words of Truth. It is the higher teaching that makes a reality of the theory you have read. It is available to you here and now. Its name is practice.

Whenever I am faced with something that seems beyond me, I remember the two little girls with the seemingly impossible feat to perform. And I know that I, too, can succeed. The secret of success? Its name is practice.

One + One = One

Mathematics has been called the science of relationships, for through it the various departments of the separate sciences are related in a logical pattern of understanding. Mathematics has been defined as the science that draws necessary conclusions. We can obtain concrete and statistical knowledge of the world through the computations of mathematics, based on the necessary conclusion that one plus one always equals two.

Now the truth as Jesus taught it is also the science of relationships. It relates all the elements of life in a logical pattern of understanding. It, too, draws necessary conclusions. And we can obtain knowledge of the inner world, the spiritual realm, through basing our thinking on the necessary conclusion that one plus one equals *one*. The necessary conclusion on which we base our faith is that we and God equal one.

We have thought of ourselves as separate, as praying to God, when all the time it remains a matter of unity. What God is, we are. Back of all that appears is a spiritual sameness, a state of being one.

The number *one* denotes unity. Think about this. Unity, oneness. Unity means oneness. Not God and you adding up to two, but God and you, *one*.

What can this idea mean to us? It is revolutionary when we truly grasp it. It gives meaning to our affirmations. It makes them logical. For we see clearly that we are not praying to a separate being, we are affirming our oneness with God, with all that God is. This is the great spiritual Truth that Jesus revealed. *"I and the Father are one"* (John 10:30).

"I in them and thou in me, that they may become perfectly one" (John 17:23).

What we are one with, we are. Our need is

to discover what God is, then we know what we are.

God is light. To know that we are one with God is to affirm that we are one with light, that we are light. *"I have come as light into the world"* (John 12:46).

"You are the light of the world" (Matt. 5:14).

God is love. It follows logically that we can affirm: *I am love, for I am one with God.*

God is life. We do not pray for God to bring life to us, rather we know and affirm: *I am life.*

God is substance. God is. We are. What is our need? Our need is to know God, for in knowing God we come to know the ultimate Truth, the ultimate reality, that there is no separation. *I and the Father are one.* This is the divine unity. This is the oneness that is health to our bodies, light to our minds, peace to our souls.

I am one with God. This is the necessary conclusion that begins and ends our search for Truth. One plus one equals one. God and us equal not two but one.

If You Know These Things

There are many persons who endlessly seek the mystery beyond the mystery, who go from teacher to teacher, from course to course, trying to find a secret formula that will give them entrance into the inner kingdom. Sometimes, because Truth seems so simple, so clear, they will have none of it, or else they will persist in trying to discover what is being kept hidden from them.

The teachings of Unity are clear and simple and understandable, like the teachings of Jesus. And like the teachings of Jesus, they must be practiced in order to be effective.

We may know what all the books say. We may be able to quote Truth principles. How-

ever, we do not *know* the Truth until we have
practiced it, until we have made the theories
come alive in our experiences.

Sometimes a person will say, "I know all
that. I know all about Truth." But such a person is very often at a loss to know how to
meet some practical problem of life. He may
know all about Truth but he does not know
how to use it.

Jesus said: *"If you know these things,
blessed are you if you do them"* (John 13:17).

Sometimes we think of practical and mystical as being directly opposite. We may think
of practical as being matter-of-fact. It is the
use of Truth ideas, the practice of them, that
opens the way to the greatest mystical reve-
lations. To practice Truth is to experience it.
To practice the presence of God is to experience it, and this is the most mystical experience of all.

Practical Christianity may seem to some
persons to take a most impractical stand, if
by practical they think of facing the facts as
they seem and saying: "This is the way
things are. Nothing can be done about them."
Practical Christianity says: "This is the way

things are to surface appearances. But beyond the appearance is the underlying goodness of God. There is always a way to change, to improve, to transform anything, any condition. God is present in and through all, and with God all things are possible."

Prayer is practical. Prayer is putting into practice all that we believe. Prayer is putting mind, heart, and spirit in tune with God. Prayer is lifting up our thoughts to a higher level. Prayer is stilling anxieties and fears. Prayer is a way of listening to Spirit within us; it is a way of releasing the God-powers and energies that are within us.

Prayer produces practical results. Prayer changes us. Prayer changes our lives. Prayer affects everything about us. Through prayer, Truth ideas come alive in us, take root in us, grow in our minds, thrive in our hearts, flourish in our lives.

When we make affirmations, it may seem to some that we are trying to fool ourselves, that we are making statements that are contrary to fact. They may point to affirmations and ask, "Do you call them practical?"

Affirmations are not only practical, they

are imperative for most of us. Most of us are easily deceived by the appearance of things. We think we are being practical when actually we are being negative, even pessimistic, about ourselves and our lives.

Affirmations are neither to bolster our courage nor to try to make us think that something is true that is not true. They are principles that we hold up before our minds to remind ourselves what Truth really is. Are we sick, do we feel weak and lifeless? This may be a fact, but it is not the truth about us.

Affirmations transform the character of our thinking and feeling by directing our thoughts Godward. But more than this, affirmations stand as a perfect idea that is true, that always has been true, that always will be true. Conditions change, we pass through many experiences, but the unchanging Truth about us is that first and foremost we are spiritual beings, created in God's own image. When we affirm this and stand with it, we break old patterns of negative thinking and emerge into a new expression of life.

Practical Christianity helps us to see beyond the surface to the perfect goodness of

God that is always present. Through the very practical way we use Truth in our everyday experiences, we discover the great and wonderful power of God that lies within us.

We can all be advanced Truth students. Truth comes alive in us and for us as we practice and use it day by day.

A Good Medicine

Charles Fillmore, co-founder of Unity, when conducting meetings must often have realized what a serious and intent audience he faced, for these people before him came not to be entertained but to be helped and healed. They came seeking life itself. They came seeking and expecting to find new light and understanding.

Mr. Fillmore must have thought many times of these words from Proverbs as he looked at the strained, tense faces of his audience: *A cheerful heart is a good medicine* (Prov. 17:22), for he never failed to put his audience in a relaxed and cheerful frame of mind. He helped them to be receptive to great truths by lightening their hearts with little humorous stories.

When we are earnestly seeking spiritual enlightenment and understanding, when we have some great need of healing or supply or emotional control, it might be well for us to imagine that we are Truth teachers looking out over the audience of our thoughts. We see our needs and desires from a different perspective when we do this. We are better able to be objective in our view. Like an understanding Truth teacher, we are not condemnatory or intolerant toward our thoughts because they are so strained and unhappy, so confused and bewildered. We look upon them with compassion. We are able to give them the good medicine they need: faith, understanding, and the assurance of God's unfailing help. We are able to inspire them, to lift them up, to help them see many reasons for believing in God's goodness. We are able to teach our thoughts to let go of despair, we are able to inject new life into them, to put new spirit into them. We are the cheerful heart that can minister to our own distressed thoughts and emotions.

Every day Unity receives hundreds of letters telling about the wonderful results that have been accomplished through faith and prayer. It is indeed a cheerful heart that can write as one woman wrote recently: "For the first time I know what it means to be a loved and protected child of the Most High. I thank you, dear friends, for your holy prayers, which He on high must delight to answer. Never have I felt such peace, such happiness, such security!"

We can begin teaching and helping our thoughts and emotions at any time. We are never too old or too young to learn spiritual truths.

In speaking about the help she has found through Unity a young woman says: "I am indeed fortunate in having discovered Unity while I am young. Now I have a lifetime before me to reap the benefits of your wonderful work." Another woman tells how she revolutionized her thinking at the age of 77. At 80 she looks back on her three years of spiritual experience and says that Truth teachings have transformed what she had feared would be a boring old age into a cheerful, joyous, fulfilling new age!

It might seem that a person with a mental disorder would be beyond help, would not be able to take control of his thoughts and emotions, but this is not true. Unity has many reports of persons who have found sanity and peace of mind through discovering their spiritual nature, through discovering the overcoming power in themselves.

There was a woman who had suffered a nervous breakdown and had been confined in a state institution. Someone sent her Unity literature, and through the Unity teachings she gradually began to find her way back to normality. Through these teachings she learned that she had the power to overcome fear, jealousy, and suspicion. She found her true self; she was able to be loving and forgiving in her heart. When this sense of inner freedom came, she knew that she would be released from the hospital, as she shortly was.

Silent Unity conducts healing meetings at which they pray for all the people who turn to them for help. In a sense, when we pray individually, we conduct healing meetings. The members of our healing meetings are our thoughts, which pass on the message of Truth and light to our emotions, even to the cells of our bodies. Every part of us feels the uplifting power of our prayers; every part of us rejoices in our realization of oneness with God.

In a sense, if we think of our prayer period as a healing meeting for our thoughts, we accomplish far more, for we are able to take spiritual control as a spiritual leader. We do not wander away with the truant thoughts; we do not fear with the fearful thoughts; we do not weep with the sorrowing thoughts; we do not doubt with the skeptical thoughts. We stand with the Christ nature, with God's Spirit in us, and we are able to uplift and instruct and guide our thoughts.

To the wandering thoughts we say, *"Stand firm, and see the salvation of the Lord"* (Exod. 14:13). To the fearful thoughts we say: *There is nothing to fear. God is our defense and our deliverance.* To the sorrowing thoughts we say: *"Let not your hearts be troubled, neither let them be afraid"* (John 14:27). *"Lo, I am with you always"* (Matt. 28:20). To the doubting thoughts we say,

"Put me to the test . . . if I will not open the windows of heaven for you and pour down for you an overflowing blessing" (Mal. 3:10).

You can teach Truth to your thoughts, you can teach cheerfulness to your heart, for you are one with the very Spirit of God, who is all wisdom, all love, all life, all power!

Fearless in Life,
Fearless in Death

Friends and relatives move away, perhaps halfway around the world. We may never see them again, but we do not grieve. We know where they are, we feel assured about them. We miss them, of course, but we know that they must be where they are and carry on their lives where they are. We are separated physically, but we feel our oneness though we are miles, even oceans, apart.

Some years ago a close and dear friend had been told that she did not have much longer to live. She said to me reassuringly, "It will be just as though I have gone on a long trip." She believed that her work here was finished and that it was time for her to move on. When

she passed I deeply missed her and wished
that she could have stayed with us longer.
Still I was able to find comfort in the thought
that she was on a journey, that it was not
death but another phase of life itself that she
was entering. Her confident faith in God and
in life sustained all of us who knew her and
made us better people, inspired us to give
more to life, to make life more meaningful for
ourselves and for others as well.

The fear of death is overcome as our fear of
living is overcome. If we are fearful of everything else, then death is no exception. The
more we overcome little fears, the more we
dare to live fully, the more we make every day
a day in which we give of ourselves to life and
to others, the more we are able to cope with
the fear of death. We find life so good that we
know whatever the future may hold will be
good also.

We can develop such a confident trust in
God, we can so increase our faith in the never-
failing presence of God that even in the face
of death we have faith, we are fearless. We
know that God's love is with us and our dear
ones, that though all things change, life is

eternal. We see beyond the human self to the God-created Christ self which is indestructible, deathless, perfect.

We have faith to believe that life is more than a span of a few years, that our life did not begin with birth nor does it end with death. We always have been and always will be a part of life, though the how or why may yet remain a mystery. But life itself is a mystery: *For now we see in a mirror dimly* (I Cor. 13:12).

Fearless in life, fearless in death, we can release those who depart the scene and see them moving forward, attaining spiritual stature, fulfilling their Christ identity. Though they have gone beyond our sight and hearing, we are always and forever one with them in spirit, one with them in the love of God.

For I am sure that neither death, nor life, nor angels, nor principalities, nor things present, nor things to come, nor powers, nor height, nor depth, nor anything else in all creation, will be able to separate us from the love of God in Christ Jesus our Lord (Rom. 8:38, 39).

These words give us a marvelous base for fearless living. Come what may, challenged though we may be by the vicissitudes of life, there is nothing to fear. We can never be separated from the love of God!

My Own Shall Come to Me

When we see the word *justice* we may think of lawmakers, the Supreme Court, the Constitution, all that makes up the concept of justice in a legal sense—court cases, lawsuits, legal entanglements.

Or the word *justice* may evoke the thought of a judgment day. We may think of justice in terms of punishment and reward.

Whatever thought the word *justice* evokes, it may seem only an abstract idea unless we run up against a situation in our life that seems unjust. Or it may be that we are not personally involved but are moved and concerned because of apparent injustice inflicted upon someone else. Then we want justice; we pray that justice will be done.

This is when it is important that we have a strong and solid belief in the divine law of justice, the law that is above and beyond man-made law, the law that always assures the right outworking of all things.

The idea of justice needs to be based on the truth that God's law of justice is always at work, that ultimately, despite appearances, God's law of justice always prevails.

The idea of justice needs to be based, too, on the truth that no one can usurp our place, that no one can take away our good, that our own comes to us under divine law. This realization sets us free from unhappy comparisons of ourselves with others. This realization helps us to know that we are beloved of God and have our own important place and part to fill in the world.

Have you ever known a person who felt that the world was against him, who felt that he was unjustly treated, who believed that others were taking advantage of him? A feeling of being unjustly treated can build up in us, sometimes without our being consciously aware of it. There are persons who always feel that everyone fares better than they.

There is a story of the little boy who said, as his mother cut a piece of cake, "All that for Grandma?" The mother said, "No, this is your piece." "For me?" said the little boy. "Oh, what a little piece!" The idea of being unfairly treated can begin when we are little children. Once I was at a family birthday party. The little girl, who was eight, had a cake with candles. Her little brother, age five, whose birthday had been celebrated just a few weeks previously, felt unjustly treated because he did not have a cake this time too.

Sometimes adults carry along these childish feelings. They feel unfairly treated and left out if someone else has something they want or think they want.

Do you remember the parable of the prodigal son, how the elder brother felt unfairly treated and sulked and refused to go into the house where there was merrymaking because of his younger brother's return? He complained to his father that he had been a loyal son, he had stayed home, he had not shirked his responsibilities. Now, his brother who had wasted his inheritance in riotous living was being treated like a homecoming hero—a gold ring for his finger, the fatted calf for a feast.

But the father said to the elder son, "Son, you are always with me, and all that is mine is yours."

This is what we need to realize. No one can take our place. We can rejoice in the good fortune of others, we can wish others well, we can know that God's love is broad enough, understanding enough so that no one is ever left out. We are never overlooked, never left out. All that the Father has is ours.

I heard someone say recently, half jokingly, "I don't want what I deserve!" Well, this kind of remark reveals a feeling of unworthiness, a feeling that we should in some way be punished. What we deserve as children of God is only the best. God's will is good. As we accept the idea of love as the law of justice, we shall feel under the law of love and know that we are not bound or limited or held back by what we have thought of as unfair or unjust conditions. John Burroughs wrote these beautiful lines:

Serene I fold my hands and wait,
   Nor care for wind, nor tide, nor sea;

I rave no more 'gainst time or fate,
For lo, my own shall come to me.
Rather than rail against injustice, rather than feel unfairly or unjustly treated, let us lift up our thoughts and feelings, let us lift up our faith.

We are beloved of God. Our own comes to us under divine law. God's law of justice and harmony is always at work in all situations.

Do Not Believe It

What we believe is important; and what we do not believe is also important. We need both to affirm and deny in our thoughts and prayers. There are times when we need to take a definite stand and say in the face of fear of some condition or experience: *I do not believe in you!*

Even a person who is faithful in prayer and filled with a strong sense of God's presence and power may not be completely free from fearful beliefs or from fearful suggestions made by others.

If there is something we long to do, if we feel urged to develop latent talents and powers and either say to ourselves or someone else says to us, "It is too late to begin again," let us fearlessly declare: *I do not believe it! It is never too late to express God or to call forth the powers and abilities with which I was created.*

If we ever feel unloved, unwanted, or alone, let us say to ourselves: *I do not believe it! I am never alone, for I am forever one with God. God loves me with an everlasting love. Through the love of God I attract love to myself. Through knowing that I am loved, I am able to radiate love and happiness into the lives of others.*

If we are fearful of getting old, let us deny this fear. Let us say: *I do not believe it! I am one with the eternal, inexhaustible life of Spirit. My strength is renewed; my youth is renewed. The life of God in me is ageless, unending.*

If ever we are inclined to think that other persons are working against us, that we are being unjustly treated, let us say to ourselves: *I do not believe it! There is no criticism or condemnation in me, for me, or against me. I am under the law of divine love and only good and justice can manifest in my life experiences.*

If we long to change but are fearful of change, let us rid our minds of fear. Let us say to the thought that change is something to fear: *I do not believe it! God is with me through every change. I have a free and flexible mind and spirit. I am not bound by old thoughts and old ways. I am on an upward path, supported by God's loving presence. I am a new creature in Christ.*

If we are pressed for time and think that we do not have time to do the things we need or want to do, let us remind ourselves of the truth by saying to this belief in lack of time: *I do not believe it! I have all the time there is. No one has more time than I have. There is no lack of time. I now give thanks for order in my life, order in my thinking, and order in my affairs. I know that as I let God work through me I have time to accomplish, easily and perfectly, all that is required of me.*

If we are in bondage to some habit from which we long to be free, but feel that it is impossible for us to quit it, let us declare: *I do not believe it! Greater is he that is in me than he that is in the world. The Spirit in me is*

*greater than any habit. The Spirit in me now
sets me free. I fearlessly take my stand for
freedom, and I have mastery and perfect control.*

If we have moments of depression and feel
that we are unimportant or unworthy, let us
reject this feeling. Let us say: *I do not believe
it! I am God's beloved child in whom He is
well pleased. I am important to God and to
God's plan of creation.*

If things do not work out the way we had
hoped and we are tempted to give up, to admit failure, let us say to our doubts and fears:
*I do not believe it! Even though I cannot see
just how things are going to work out, I know
that all things are working together for good
and for success, for God is working in me and
through me.*

If ever we feel that some difficult situation
is impossible of solution, let us declare: *I do
not believe it! All things are possible with
God!*

If a pronouncement of "incurable" has
been given, let us stand firm in our faith. Let
us fearlessly say: *I do not believe it! God is
able to heal any and all disease!*

If we think of ourselves as inheriting negative conditions of mind or body, let us say to
ourselves: *I do not believe it! God is the one
source of all, and my inheritance is from God.
I inherit only life and strength and health. I
inherit only a perfect mind and body from
God.*

If ever we are dismayed by the prophets of
doom and fall into the thought that the world
is getting worse, that we shall all be de-
stroyed, let us fearlessly declare: *I do not
believe it! This is God's world, and God is in
charge of it. All things are under God's love
and protection, and there is nothing to fear.
God is eternal, unchanging good, and God
is with us forever, our guide, our help, our
strength.*

In every experience in life we have to take
our stand; we have to have courage to say to
fear, "I do not believe in you!" We have to
have faith to affirm that we believe in God, in
God's power, God's goodness. Let us remember that we are God's children, created in
God's image and likeness. Let us remember
that with God all things are possible and that
God's power working through us strengthens

and heals our bodies, enriches and blesses our affairs, and harmonizes and transforms our lives.

To anything less than God or good, let us say fearlessly: *I do not believe in you!*

Even if Your Heart
Condemns You

True healing is the healing of the whole person. We are threefold beings—spirit, soul, and body—and what affects one phase of being affects all three. We work for a partial healing if we pray only for the body.

If I have a pain or an ache in my body, I know that something is wrong physically. But I need to go beyond the obvious to have a complete healing, for how I feel is not always a true indication of what is wrong. As far as my feeling goes, only my body may seem sick, whereas actually my body may be telling me in its own way that it is expressing a sick state of mind that I do not consciously realize I possess.

Without being aware of it I may be deceiving myself with false ideas about myself. I may be striving for achievements that are not in keeping with my natural abilities. I may be trying to live a life that is foreign to my true nature. I may be imitating other persons instead of expressing myself. I may be harboring feelings of fear or hate or jealousy. I may be filled with self-condemnation and feelings of unworthiness. So without knowing it I may have set up conflicts and frustrations inside myself that cause body, soul, and spirit to cry out in protest.

The protest of the body is most easily recognized, for we cannot ignore or deny or repress the pains of the body as we do the pains of the soul and spirit. It is right that we should work to heal the body, to overcome the pain, but we should also work for the restoration of our souls, for the healing of our minds, for the overcoming of our inner conflicts and frustrations if we would know true healing.

The way to do this is to know the truth about ourselves. *"You will know the truth, and the truth will make you free"* (John 8:32).

The truth about us is that we are more than just a body and a mind; we are spiritual beings, endowed with the power of the Most High. God's own Spirit is in us, and God's will for us is good beyond anything we can imagine for ourselves. Humanly we may fall short, but always God sees us as spiritual beings.

Our feelings do not always tell us the truth. Because you have felt that you were a certain kind of person for a good many years does not necessarily mean that this is true. You may have believed yourself to be lacking in intelligence or ability; you may have felt that you were unloved and unworthy; you may have felt that happiness was not for you. Whatever you have believed about yourself that made you feel unworthy, uncertain, unwanted, or inadequate is not true, no matter how much the opinion of other persons seems to confirm it. Your heart may condemn you, but God in you knows only the truth about you.

If our feelings have misled our minds, it is not illogical to believe that our feelings mislead our bodies, too. If I am sick, it may be because of "something I ate"; probably it is because of something I felt or thought.

True healing is healing of the whole person—spirit, soul, and body. True healing is the result of consciously knowing the truth about ourselves, the truth that we are spiritual beings, created in God's image and likeness, whole, pure, perfect, sinless, deathless.

Your Soul Chooses Largely

"You did not choose me, but I chose you"
(John 15:16). It helps me to believe that life is
more than a combination of circumstances,
that things do not happen by chance. It helps
me to believe that the Christ Spirit in me has
chosen a way of progress and unfoldment for
me, even though humanly I may not understand how the events and circumstances of
my life have any spiritual significance.

In one sense I consciously make my choice
in life. I decide for this course of action, I
decide against that one. But it must be that
my soul makes choices that are beyond my
conscious volition. If I believe that nothing
happens by chance, then it must follow that

the soul of me chose birth at an appointed time, in an appointed place. Consciously I did not choose to be born, I did not choose the date of my birth, I did not choose my parents or my brothers and sisters. But I believe that I am what I am, I am where I am for a reason, and that my soul, with knowledge beyond my conscious reasoning power, chose with unerring wisdom the path of this, my human life.

You did not choose me, but I chose you. The Christ in us says this to us, even as Jesus said it to His disciples. Before we consciously knew or heard about Christ, His Spirit had chosen us as a dwelling place. *"Before Abraham was, I am"* (John 8:58). Before we were born we were spiritually identified with Christ.

There are many things in life that we experience, though not by choice. When we have something difficult to meet we wonder why we must meet it. We would, if we could, choose something far different in the way of experiences. It must be that in ways we do not understand our soul makes its choices; and what the soul chooses it is capable of meeting. In ourselves we may feel that a situation is beyond us, that we cannot possibly meet it, but there is something in us that is always capable, ready to meet anything that confronts us. The soul is seeking fulfillment, it is seeking oneness with Christ. Sometimes the most trying experiences are the ones through which our soul is developed the most, in which we come the closest to a consciousness of ourselves as spiritual beings.

Have you ever wondered about the reason for things? Have you wondered why you are where you are in life, why you are doing what you are doing, why your life seems to have taken the turn it has? Even though you cannot answer these questions from a human standpoint—that is, not really answer them— you can find a satisfactory answer in the realization of the truth about yourself. If you realize that you are a spiritual being, a living soul sent out from God, that your life is without beginning or end, you can begin to see yourself and the events of your life from a different perspective. You are essentially a spiritual being, but you are at the same time a human being. Your journey in life is toward the spiritual, toward the complete renewal and spiritualization of mind, soul, and body.

As a human being you may seem far from the goal of spiritual perfection, but human reasoning cannot tell you either how far or how near you are to it. Spiritual things must be spiritually perceived. Spirit in you, Christ in you, tells you that you are God's beloved child. Spirit in you knows your need for growth, for understanding, and Spirit in you says "well done" when an overcoming is made. You may not even have realized your own need, but the experiences of your life seemed almost to force you to call forth qualities of mind and heart and soul that you did not even know you possessed.

Sometimes the choice of the soul seems a more demanding one than any we would consciously make ourselves. Humanly we often feel limited, inadequate; we feel that we are as nothing, that other persons are more blessed, more endowed with talent, more able to give something worthwhile to the world. But the soul chooses largely for us. The soul's choices are not limited by lack of education or family background or money or any of the many lacks that seem to frustrate our human desire for achievement.

The soul chooses largely because it knows that Christ has chosen it and appointed it to go forth. Where humanly we are afraid, the soul fearlessly chooses to walk through the very *"valley of the shadow of death,"* for it knows neither life nor death, but only progress.

If you are at a place in your life where you cannot understand why you have to meet the things you have to meet, know that there is a divine reason behind every human happening. No matter what the experiences you have to meet, you are more than equal to them in your divine nature. Your soul has chosen the particular path your life is taking because it is the path that leads out of darkness into light. Christ in you makes you more than conqueror in all things.

Believe this, act from this belief, and you will stand triumphant in every trial, you will meet and overcome every difficulty, you will go forward with glory.

You Have Freedom of Choice

The word *choose* comes from a Latin word *qustare,* meaning to taste. In Job we read:

> *"For the ear tests words*
> *as the palate tastes food.*
> *Let us choose what is right;*
> *let us determine among ourselves*
> *what is good."*

(Job 34:3, 4)

To choose means to select, especially to select freely and after consideration. Choice is an opportunity of choosing freely.

Moses said to the children of Israel: *"I have set before you life and death, blessing and curse; therefore choose life, that you . . . may live"* (Deut. 30:19).

Joshua said to the children of Israel: *"And if you be unwilling to serve the Lord, choose this day whom you will serve . . . as for me and my house, we will serve the Lord" . . . And the people said to Joshua, "Nay; but we will serve the Lord." Then Joshua said to the people, "You are witnesses against yourselves that you have chosen the Lord, to serve him"* (Josh. 24:15, 21, 22).

In Isaiah we read: *"He shall eat curds and honey when he knows how to refuse the evil and choose the good"* (Isa. 7:15).

In Psalms 119:30 we read: *I have chosen the way of faithfulness.*

And Jesus said to Martha, who was upset and anxious about many things, that she needed to choose the *good portion,* as Mary had done.

Life is really a matter of choices. Robert Frost says in his poem, "The Road Not Taken":

Two roads diverged in a wood, and I—
I took the one less traveled by,
And that has made all the difference.

We come to many crossroads, many turning points in our journey through life. Which road shall we take? The choice is up to us.

Charles Fillmore says: *We can be what we determine to be. We can be masters or we can be serfs. It rests with us whether we shall fill the high places in life or the low, whether we shall serve or be served, lead or be led, or be sickly or healthy.*

This is the crux of the Unity teachings, that we do have a choice, that we not only have a choice but we have the God-given power to change our thinking, to change our lives through our freedom of choice.

Unity often hears from people who tell us that their way of life has been changed because of the new understanding that has come to them. They see themselves in a new light. They feel their oneness with God, their oneness with God's presence and power. When we take the road of Truth, when we choose to follow our inner guidance, that, as the poet has said, makes all the difference.

We may have made poor choices along the way, but we are not bound to past mistakes or failures. We can change the direction of our lives, we can choose the way of healing, success, and happiness.

I read in the newspaper about a man in his 70s who had quit school when he was ten years old. All his life he had been more or less a roustabout, a drifter. He was in a hospital recovering from surgery when he saw something on television about qualifying for the equivalent of a high school diploma. He thought to himself, "Why not?" When he got out of the hospital he found out about classes and necessary tests and began studying. He got his high school diploma equivalent and is now doing college work. He said that it has opened a new way of life and thought to him. Certainly he made a choice in the right direction, a choice that most people would have considered impossible for a man with such a background, a man of his age and place in life.

I feel that we not only make choices but we are chosen. Jesus said: *You did not choose me, but I chose you and appointed you that you should go and bear fruit and that your fruit should abide.* We are chosen to express the Christ. We may wonder why we are here, what our purpose in life is. Whether we are aware of it or not, we have been chosen to fill our own appointed part. We are where we are by divine appointment.

Charles Fillmore says: *We are all the chosen of the Lord, and we make the covenant that carries us into His visible presence by laying down the personal self and taking up the universal self. Christ it is that thunders in the depths of our souls, "Who say ye that I am?"*

We choose consciously and we choose unconsciously. Every prayer is a choice, every affirmation is a choice. *"As for me and my house, we will serve the Lord."* This is what you are saying every time you choose to have faith, every time you choose to affirm your oneness with God, your oneness with God's light, love, wisdom, and power.

At any time we can change the tenor of our thinking and thus change the tenor of our lives.

God has given us the ability to think, to learn, to use good judgment, to choose happy and effective paths in life. We have been given wonderful powers and faculties, but we need to use them. We need to draw on the innate wisdom and sound counsel within us.

As we pray to be shown what to do to bring

our lives into harmony with God's goodness, as we pray to have insight, discernment, and good judgment, we will be given the wisdom to act unerringly in ways that produce good results, in ways that bless us and bless others as well.

Freedom of choice! Let us choose the way of Truth, the way of healing, the way of success, the way of happiness.

Freedom of choice! The course we choose, the road we travel, can make all the difference.

You Are a Miracle

Have you ever felt like an ugly duckling? I have. I think that all of us have times when we feel out of step, times when we doubt our worth and ability. We may feel lonely and unloved.

A friend described her ugly duckling times as "pity parties." If we find ourselves thinking "poor me," it's time to remind ourselves as quickly as possible that this feeling of unhappiness and rejection is not the truth about us.

The ugly duckling was unhappy because he did not know what he was or what he was becoming. He wanted to be something he was not, when all the time he was destined for something more wonderful than he dreamed of or imagined possible.

The story of the ugly duckling has universal appeal because it is our story. We accept an ugly duckling image of ourselves little realizing that in spite of turns and twists and difficulties in our lives, God's Spirit in us is shaping and molding us in marvelous and wondrous ways.

I know of a woman who had every reason to feel like the ugly duckling. She was born with a condition that affected her body so that she had difficulty controlling her motions and she also had difficulty speaking so that she could be understood. But she had a bright mind and was able to hold a job that did not require meeting the public.

In her thirties she began corresponding with a pen pal in a distant state. In her letters she expressed her real self, she gave expression to her thoughts and feelings, to the joy and love that she felt in her heart. Before long, her pen pal fell in love with her. He asked her to marry him and said that he was coming to see her. She was crushed. She felt that she had deceived him, and she knew that she had to tell him the truth. She wrote to him, describing the ugly duckling version of herself that she carried with her. She asked his forgiveness and believed that she would never hear from him again. But shortly he arrived on the scene and told her that to him she was wonderful and beautiful, that he had fallen in love with the real person that she was. They subsequently married, had a child, and have enjoyed a good life. The ugly duckling was a swan after all!

To know ourselves, to see ourselves as God sees us, to believe in ourselves, to know that God believes in us, this is what we long to be able to do. On the surface our lives may seem happy and complete, but behind the scenes we may feel far from confident, we may have fears about many things. This is where we must change our inner feelings through joyous affirmation.

The highest affirmation of Truth that we can make about ourselves cannot possibly describe the glorious Christ presence in us.

Have we felt inadequate? Christ in us is our light, our wisdom, our power to do and to be. Have we felt set apart, cut off from others?

Christ in us is love that attracts, love that makes us one, love that gives us the joy and satisfaction we seek.

Do we fear change, the breaking up of things that have meant stability and substance to us? Christ in us is changeless. Christ in us knows no fear. Christ in us knows that our lives are unfolding in ways that are right and good, in ways that assure our spiritual growth, our spiritual progress.

We are blessed. God sees us as remarkable. We cannot begin to count the reasons we have for rejoicing in life, every minute of it.

Think of the miracle that you are! A person may say, "I cannot affirm that I am wonderful. It sounds so egotistical." Anyone who feels this way needs to understand what an affirmation is. An affirmation does not have to do with that which we already are. We may have much growing to do, we may have many lessons yet to learn, we may be far from perfect in our personal selves. But there is that in us which is perfect, pure, all-wise, all-loving, all-powerful. When we affirm the truth, we are affirming our oneness with absolute good, with God.

When we know the truth about ourselves—
that we are children of God with a divine purpose and destiny—we are joyous! When we
feel confident and capable, when we are using
our talents and abilities to enhance our lives
and the lives of others, we are joyous!

To you who are reading these words now,
affirm the miracle that you are, believe in the
miracle that you are. Say to yourself: *I am a
living, breathing miracle! How marvelous is
the power of Christ in me; how joyous is the
song of life in me; how soul-satisfying is the
love of Christ in me!*

You Are God's Image

Have you ever thought how dominant is the pronoun *I*? Even the most self-effacing person cannot help but do most of his thinking in terms of I. From the early age when we become conscious of ourselves as individuals each of us lives in a small world of our own, revolving around the pronoun *I*.

Since this is true, surely it is important that we have a right concept of the I in us, for it is from this focal point that our world takes shape and form. I think, I speak, I act, and my mind, my body, and my affairs follow the pattern set for them.

When Jesus Christ spoke from the consciousness of His oneness with God, He used the pronoun *I* in its highest sense. The real I in each of us is revealed as we, like Jesus Christ, realize our unity with God. *"The glory which thou has given me I have given them, that they may be one even as we are one, I in them and thou in me, that they may become perfectly one, so that the world may know that thou hast sent me and hast loved them even as thou hast loved me"* (John 17:22, 23).

All of us have at times pierced the veil of darkness, ignorance, and fear that clouds our human vision and discerned the truth that we are indeed spiritual beings, that what is eternally existent in us did not begin with this physical life, nor does it end if physical life ceases. Have you not felt the uplift and inspiration that come with the realization that there is that in you which has always been, which can never be defeated, never die? This is the greatest realization that we can have: that we are children of God, created in God's image and after God's likeness. It was this realization that gave Jesus Christ power and authority. He knew that He was the Son of God, and because of this He knew that there was nothing in the world impossible to Him.

How differently most of us would react to our daily experiences and problems if we always met them as would a child of God. We should not be hampered by fear, doubt, indecision. We should feel the power of God working through us, and we should see the power of God working through all persons and all situations. It is not really hard to act like a child of God. We do not have to stop and think how to act; we need only to follow unhesitatingly the prompting of the God-self in us. Our good, our happiness, can be small or as great as our vision permits.

We cannot say with Jesus Christ: *"I and the Father are one"* (John 10:30), and remain fearful, or timid, or self-conscious. We cannot say with Him: *"He who has seen me has seen the Father"* (John 14:9), and act foolishly or unwisely or ungracefully. We cannot say: *"I can do nothing . . . I seek not my own will but the will of him who sent me"* (John 5:30), and remain vain or egotistical or self-centered.

Like Jesus Christ we should be God-centered. Our thoughts should never be limited, negative, fearful, selfish. They will not be if

we think of ourselves as children of God. Our
world will not be narrowed to personal, selfish limits but will broaden and widen and
deepen. Day by day we can act more like children of God and less like the weak, fearful, in-
hibited human beings we have thought ourselves to be.

Some persons object to using "I" in affirmations. In all sincerity and humility they
hesitate to proclaim perfection in the personal self. But with an understanding of "I"
as God's name for us we see how very wise we
are to proclaim the perfection of God's image
in us. By doing this we become centered in
God and in the Spirit of truth. The more God-
centered we become the more we are able to
help other people, the more light we radiate.
No one can become aware of self as a child of
God without at the same time becoming
aware of his unity with all persons. We are
one mind, one heart, one Spirit. It is through
realizing our unity with God and our unity
with all persons that we live together in peace
and goodwill and enjoy the blessings of
health and happiness and plenty. *It is the
Spirit himself bearing witness with our spirit*

that we are children of God, and if children, then heirs, heirs of God and fellow heirs with Christ (Rom. 8:16, 17).

Your Youth Is Renewed

I remember my mother once saying to me: "I don't feel old! I don't feel any different inside!"

I do not believe that anyone ever feels old. A person may be eighty or ninety, but years do not affect the inner spirit, which is always young. The important part of us, the real self of us, is untouched by years; it is ever vital, youthful, eternally alive.

A friend wrote to me, saying, "Tomorrow I will be seventy years old. I can't believe it. Thank God, I am well physically; I am mentally alert; and I am able to be independent."

We may fear old age. We may dread the thought of being limited in activity, we may dread the thought of becoming a burden to our family and friends, or having to depend on society for our care and welfare. If we think along these lines, we can build up a bleak picture.

Like my mother, like my friend, we may be amazed to find that when we reach the age we had thought of as old age, we do not feel old at all! We are active, happy, busy. We feel strong and well. We lift our sights. We decide that old age has yet a while to be reached by us.

One man said that he never thought of anyone as being old unless that person was at least fifteen years older than he.

The fear of old age has little to do with years and much to do with our thought about it. The age we are is the best possible age for us, because this is where we are in our journey in life. If we have lived many years, so much the better. If we have lived just a few years, all to the good. Either way, we have much to be thankful for, much to learn, much to look forward to, and much to enjoy and participate in right now, today.

The number of years lived brings many

changes, but years in themselves do not age us nor do they change us. It is how we live our years that makes the difference. Our growing is from within, our progress is marked by upward steps in consciousness, not by dates on the calendar.

All of us have the inner feeling that we are capable of much more than we have yet expressed, and this feeling is not a mistaken one. At any age, how ageless is our vision, how ageless are our dreams!

With the passing of years, changes take place in our bodies, in our circumstances; life moves on and we move with it. But with childlike faith and in a childlike spirit, at any age we can find joy in living and we can keep alive the feeling of youth, of agelessness. It is our secret weapon against belief in old age. We can refuse to equate the number of years we have lived with ill health, with faults and failings and despair. We can remind ourselves that we are beloved children of God, now and forever.

We are spiritual beings, here for a purpose, and we are needed and important, whatever our age. Best of all, we have a youthful spirit

that is irrepressible, that time cannot quench,
that the passing of years cannot touch.

> *Bless the Lord, O my soul . . .*
> > *who crowns you with steadfast love*
> > > *and mercy,*
> > *who satisfies you with good as long as*
> > > *you live*
> > *so that your youth is renewed like the*
> > > *eagle's.*

(Psalms 103:2, 4-5)

Sing a New Song

New. What a good word! We may tell ourselves that everything is going to be different, that we are done with the past, that we
are embarking on the new. But we may soon
be caught up in the same old thoughts and
feelings and reactions. We may find ourselves
singing the same old song.

In Isaiah 42:10 it says: *Sing to the Lord a
new song.* And the Psalmist says what we
need to say to ourselves: *I will sing a new
song to thee, O God* (Psalms 144:9).

Our song is our consciousness. Our song is
the thoughts we think, the words we speak,
the feelings to which we give expression. We
may have been singing a sad song, we may

have been singing the blues, we may have been singing a song of woe. Now it is time to sing a new song—a song with new words, new music, new tempo.

As we listen in prayer and silence, God gives us new words.

> *"From this time forth I make you hear*
> *new things,*
> *hidden things which you have not*
> *known."*

(Isa. 48:6)

Sometimes when we are unhappy with ourselves and our lives, we think that the way to change is to work with what is wrong. We are not singing a new song but we are thinking about the old song and asking ourselves, "Where did I go wrong?" "Where have I failed?" "What is it in me that draws difficult experiences to me?" "Why me, God?"

The new song that is trying to sing itself through us is barely heard in the clamor of negation that may arise in us as we concentrate on all that seems to be wrong.

The past is past. The new song is there, waiting to be sung through us. We are at a point of beginning again. Old thoughts and old conditions are as waters that have passed away.

A song has words, and the new song we are singing has words—words of life, words of love, words of strength, words of power, words of peace, words of faith, words of wisdom. A song begins with an idea. The new song we are singing begins with the idea of our true nature as children of God. *Therefore, if any one is in Christ, he is a new creation; the old has passed away, behold, the new has come* (II Cor. 5:17). We change our song, we change our lives, as we let Christ be the basis for our thinking and living.

Be renewed in the spirit of your minds (Eph. 4:23). We sing a new song as we are renewed in the spirit of our minds, as we no longer let negative thoughts and feelings dominate us, as we no longer accept the belief that it is impossible for us to change, that we are bound to old ways, to old limitations.

This is the time to sing a new song, a song of health and life and wholeness. This is the time to know that old conditions can be healed, that we are new in every atom and cell of our being. This is the time to let God sing a song of life and health through us.

This is the time to sing a song of joy and peace and harmony. This is the time to release old hurts, old memories of mistakes, to release any trace of unforgiveness or bitterness. The new song of love we sing swells in majestic harmony within us. God sings a beautiful new song through us.

This is the time to sing a new song, a song of faith—faith in God, faith in Jesus Christ, faith in ourselves as children of God and joint heirs with Christ. This is the time to sing a song of confidence and courage, a song that marks us as destined for greatness and high places—greatness of spirit, high places in consciousness.

This is the time for a new song. God is giving us the words. Let us sing it!

The Stone Is Rolled Away

It wasn't a letter, and it wasn't a greeting card. It was just a piece of notepaper sent to me at Easter time from a friend. It contained one line, but that one line told the whole story: "The stone has been rolled away!"

That one-line message told the story of this friend's resurrection out of old and fearful ways of thinking; it told the story of his resurrection out of belief in lack and ill health; it told the story of his newfound freedom of spirit; it told the story of his emergence from the tomb of darkness into the light of Truth.

We may feel that it is impossible to change some condition that has become our "stone," which keeps us imprisoned, as it were. Physical effort does not move this stone; mental effort moves it. The stone is rolled away by spiritual power, the power that overcomes every obstacle, every limitation. As we let God work through us, as we trust God to show us the way of freedom and light, we are imbued with this power.

Jesus' message is a message of life, of overcoming power, of faith and answered prayer. *"I came that they may have life, and have it abundantly"* (John 10:10).

"With God all things are possible" (Matt. 19:26).

"If you have faith as a grain of mustard seed, you will say to this mountain, 'Move from here to there,' and it will move; and nothing will be impossible to you" (Matt. 17:20, 21).

Jesus did not talk about impossibilities. He did not talk about obstructions. He did not talk about immovable stones.

What have we allowed to become a stone in our consciousness? What have we allowed to shut us off from feeling vitally alive, from being radiant, free, joyous, from living life effectively, successfully?

Is the appearance of disease or ill health our stone? The stone can be rolled away! Life and healing are God's will for us, and there is nothing that can obstruct the free flow of God-life within us. Easter is a good time to affirm life and healing, to know as Jesus knew that we are meant to have life and to have it abundantly.

Let us affirm words like the following: *The glorious infusion of the more abundant life of Jesus Christ vitalizes me and I am lifted up and healed.* And let us add, *The stone has been rolled away! Thank You, Father.*

Is the stone that blocks our way the inability to assume authority over our thoughts and feelings, and subsequently, over our lives? Do we feel unable to make decisions, to turn away from thoughts that drag us down, to release habits that lessen our self-esteem?

The stone can be rolled away! *"Not by might, nor by power, but by my Spirit"* (Zech. 4:6). It is that Spirit in us that overcomes the doubts and fears that have kept us in bondage. The Spirit of God is in us, and when we call upon it we receive spiritual power and authority. Our minds are illumined; we are filled with light.

Jesus said: *"You will know the truth, and the truth will make you free"* (John 8:32). The truth we are to know in order to make our spiritual breakthrough is that through the Spirit in us we have dominion and authority. We take this dominion and authority in the inner realm of thought. The more we pray and affirm our oneness with God, the easier it is to take control of our thoughts, to take control of our feelings, our actions, our lives.

The resurrecting Spirit in us sets us free from limitations, free from negation, and we embark upon a whole new way of life. *If any one is in Christ, he is a new creation; the old has passed away, behold, the new has come.*

Let us affirm: *The resurrecting Spirit in me wipes out all darkness. Christ in me gives me dominion and authority over my inner world, and my whole being is filled with light. The stone has been rolled away! Thank You, Father.*

Perhaps the stone blocking our way is a feeling of being unworthy. We cannot seem to shake off the belief that we are under condemnation for mistakes of the past. We cannot accept forgiveness. The stone can be rolled away! We can be resurrected out of any feeling of being unforgiven.

Whenever we find ourselves thinking along depressing lines, let us remind ourselves that God loves us, that God sees us as growing, learning, unfolding. God does not count our mistakes but sees our good efforts, sees us with eyes of love. God loves us.

A wonderful affirmation to hold that will help us to accept forgiveness is: *The forgiving love of Jesus Christ reaches to the depths of my being. I am forgiven the mistakes of the past and the results of the mistakes of the past.* Then let us follow this affirmation with the realization: *The stone has been rolled away! Thank You, Father.*

Is our grief over the lack of love in our lives the stone that is blocking off our happiness? Do we feel lost because someone whom we had come to depend upon is no longer a part of our lives? Do we feel that we can never be happy again? The stone can be rolled away! We can find peace of mind; our hearts can be comforted. We can be happy, though relationships change, though we can no longer continue in a way of life that seemed so right and satisfying.

Always there is new good to be experienced, new challenges to be met that call forth the best in us. Always there are new ways of sharing our lives with others and of adding to their happiness. New joy is at hand. We do not want to, nor should we, stay in an unhappy or sad state of mind. We can begin again. We can be resurrected out of hurts and unhappiness into a beautiful way of life.

Let us affirm: *I welcome the good that life has to offer. I give thanks for all that has gone before, for all those who have been a lovely part of my life, and for all those who now wait to enter the circle of my love. The stone has been rolled away! Thank You, Father.*

God Has Not Given You
a Spirit of Timidity

God did not give us a spirit of timidity. It is we who allow the spirit of timidity to build up in us. It may begin early in childhood when we feel overpowered by an older brother or sister, or when we feel lost and scared in school, surrounded by strange children, overseen by a formidable person called a teacher.

Fear of being laughed at, of saying the wrong thing, of being rejected—all add to our shyness and timidity, which we cover up by withdrawing into ourselves, by trying to let others know how we feel. Others may think of us as standoffish; they may even think of us as hostile because our defenses are always up.

We do not have to remain in a fearful, timid

state of mind. We have the power to free ourselves from this self-made prison. We have the power to be the confident, outgoing, friendly person we long to be. God has given us a spirit of power and of love, but the power must be used, the love must be expressed.

"Practice makes perfect" is the old but true saying. We can overcome fear and timidity through practice. Every day presents at least one opportunity to practice being friendly and outgoing. This does not mean that someone else will offer us the opportunity. We cannot wait for others to initiate the overcoming we need to make. We cannot wait for others to make us feel more at ease. We cannot wait for others to encourage us. Every day, in some way, we can make the effort, take the step, initiate the response that is loving and friendly and outgoing on our part.

It may be something as simple as smiling at the person in front of us at the check-out counter in the supermarket; it may be something as ordinary as picking up the telephone and calling someone to say, "I'm thinking of you." It may be something as simple as inviting a neighbor in for a cup of coffee. Little things, yes, but big steps for anyone who feels shy and withdrawn.

A friend who said, "Yesterday I walked down the street by myself," was reporting a big overcoming, for she has been too timid and fearful to leave her house, to make contact with people. Her simple act of walking down the street marked her point of freedom, the point at which she realized the nothingness of her fears. It was a turning point in her life.

Fear not. There is nothing to fear. You are loved, you live in a friendly world. You are one in spirit with the people in your world.

God has not given you a spirit of timidity. You can be the friendly, outgoing person you long to be, the person you really are.

Live Happily Ever After

Life is a continuing story. As children we liked the stories that ended, "and so they all lived happily ever after."

Isn't this what we really want to do: to live happily ever after? After the struggle, after the loss, after the unhappy time?

Happily ever after—the perfect ending to the story. But in our life story there are really no endings. What seems like an ending turns out to be a beginning. It is the conclusion of an experience; it is the beginning of a new experience.

We think some situation will never change, that some person will never change. We want everything and everyone to remain the same, happily ever after.

Happily ever after does not mean a static state, does not mean that the perfect moment, the perfect love, the perfect experience will somehow be set in time, never to change, to remain always the same, forever after.

Once I read something about Robert E. Lee that impressed me. He suffered great defeat when the south lost the Civil War; but what seemed like a sad ending was a happily ever after one. He was elected president of Washington College in Virginia and became an educator who had a profound and good influence on the lives of many people.

The story of Charles and Myrtle Fillmore, the co-founders of Unity, is a happily-ever-after one, although before they found Truth it would hardly have seemed so. They were middle-aged people with children. Myrtle was seriously ill and had been told that she had about six months to live. Charles, because of a childhood accident, had a crippled hip and had to walk with a brace. The bottom had dropped out of the real estate business and they were in desperate financial straits. But one affirmation of Truth changed the whole picture for them.

I am a child of God and therefore I do not inherit sickness was the ending of old beliefs in sickness and lack; it was the beginning of a new journey in Truth that was to bring the Fillmores healing and was to inspire them to reach out and share their light and truth with others. The faith of the Fillmores continues to help people everywhere to live happily ever after.

Think of Paul with his great change of heart, his conversion to Christianity. Certainly no one who knew him before this would have expected that he would live happily ever after, espousing the cause of Jesus Christ and doing more than probably any other person to bring the teachings of Jesus Christ to the world. Paul said, in effect, "The end is just the beginning."

But one thing I do, forgetting what lies behind and straining forward to what lies ahead, I press on toward the goal for the prize of the upward call of God in Christ Jesus (Phil. 3:13, 14).

Most of us think of Dickens' Scrooge in "A Christmas Carol" as symbolizing all that is mean and miserly; but Dickens said that after Scrooge's dream of Christmas past, Christmas present, and Christmas to come, Scrooge changed and you could not find a kinder, more generous, happier man in all of England. He lived happily ever after.

Palm Sunday, even though it seems a day of acclaim for Jesus because of the crowds and hosannas and palm branches spread in His path, is not a happily-ever-after day if we look ahead to Good Friday and the Crucifixion. But happily-ever-after triumphed over tragedy, with Jesus' resurrection from death to life.

Jesus and the Crucifixion hardly seems a happily-ever-after experience. But it was. It was the ultimate happy ending, for it proved the triumph of life over death; it showed us the way of immortal life; it raised the whole human race to a new level of consciousness.

We can live happily ever after through every experience because of Christ in us, our triumphant spirit, our hope of glory.

When we are going through a dark experience, we may wonder why. We may not see how we can meet it or ever be happy again.

But the resurrection spirit in us reaches for the light and will not let us give up or lose hope.

This too shall pass. We shall live happily ever after.

We live lifetimes within lifetimes. We change and grow. We leave our outgrown shells behind, like the chambered nautilus in Oliver Wendell Holmes' famous poem. We find our way to light and freedom.

Build thee more stately mansions, O my
*   soul,*
*   As the swift seasons roll! . . .*
Let each new temple, nobler than the last,
Shut thee from heaven with a dome more
*   vast,*
*   Till thou at length art free,*
Leaving thine outgrown shell by life's
*   unresting sea!*

We have many ever-afters in our lives. We go through many overcomings. We would not have it otherwise if we really think about it, for life is growth and change, and we want to grow, to change, to be all that we can be, to fulfill our divine potential. We cannot do this by static living.

I have known many people who lived happily ever after. There were those who thought that the end of the world had come when a marriage failed, but it hadn't. Their world seemed about to collapse around them, but it didn't. They were able to pick up the pieces of their lives, to adjust to change, to build a new life.

Sometimes with the collapse of a happily-ever-after state of living, we find how strong we are, how much life holds for us. We can look back on the time that seemed to be the death of our dreams and hopes, and give thanks. We did not just survive the experience, we actually lived happily ever after.

Sometimes we resent and resist change that seems thrust upon us. We do not want to alter the set pattern of our lives. We want things to remain the same; we want people to remain the same. We think we can live happily ever after only if nothing changes. But of course there is change. We change; life changes; people around us change. We may be trying to meet life in the same way that we did, say twenty years ago. But we are different persons, with different conditions to meet. We live happily ever after as we realize this.

If life has gone stale or sour, if we are disappointed in ourselves, if we do not feel there is much to look forward to, we may fall into self-destructive ways. We do not like life or ourselves. Consciously or unconsciously we fall into ways that rob us of our peace of mind, our health, that add to our depression and unhappiness. But always the happily-ever-after ending is possible. Always we can begin again.

We hear from people who tell us that with God's help they have found their way out of depression, out of drug addiction, out of alcoholism. They tell us that though they had lost everything—husband, wife, home, job— now they have made a new beginning. They are on the happily-ever-after path.

People meet all kinds of experiences—sickness, poverty, unhappy human relations, divorce, bereavement, situations that seem unfair and unjust. But they come through them. One time a friend, commiserating with another friend, said, "My you have been through a lot." The friend replied, "No, I have *come* through a lot."

The fairy tale began, "Once upon a time" and ended, "and so they all lived happily ever after." Our life is a continuing story that has many once-upon-a-times, many happily-ever-afters. Day after day, chapter after chapter, our story unfolds. When we are going through some difficult experience we may wonder why, we may wonder if we shall find our way. Looking back on the experience, we see that it was part of our continuing story, that it too had its happily-ever-after conclusion.

And so we live happily ever after.

You Are Not Alone

Most young people can hardly wait to be on their own. They instinctively feel great powers and possibilities within themselves; they have high hopes and dreams. Yet these same persons a few years later may be very unhappy at the thought of being on their own. A loss of someone on whom they have come to depend, perhaps the trauma of divorce, leaves them feeling vulnerable and alone.

Being on our own does not mean being deserted. It does not mean that we are without help. It does not mean that we are alone.

Being on their own is rightly perceived by the young as important to growth, important to maturity, important to the expression of their God-given powers and possibilities.

In a sense, we always are and always must be on our own. No one else can think for us; no one else can meet life for us; no one else can know our inner longings, desires, and goals. So even when we say, "But I don't want to be on my own," still it is what we must be.

We can be on our own but not alone. While in a sense we are always on our own, there is also a sense in which we are never on our own. There is never a time when we have only our human resources on which to depend.

Even when we are on our own, we have God's power within us; we have God's Spirit always with us. To know this makes the difference between being downed by circumstances or being filled with a feeling of strength and confidence in our ability to carry on and to rise above self-doubts and fears.

There are those who are faced with some difficult decision. They may ask the advice of others and may find that another person is able to shed some light on the matter. But still the final decision cannot be made by anyone else. This is where prayer helps a person to be on his own, to make his own decisions in a positive and effective manner. When we ask others for guidance, we may get glimmerings of light. When we turn to God's Spirit within us and open our minds to divine guidance, we are flooded with light. *In thy light do we see light* (Psalms 36:9). We are on our own in the truest sense, for we stand in the light of Truth, we act from the high level of Truth, we respond to life as spiritual beings, filled with God's power, strengthened by God's Spirit, guided by God's light. We are on our own, but not alone. We are able to make decisions easily and fearlessly, for we are following our inner light.

There are persons who are thrust into some situation which they do not feel qualified to handle, who feel left on their own and very much alone. Sometimes they find themselves without guidelines; there is no one to tell them what they are to do.

We may be on our own in a situation, but we are never alone. Even if there is no one to tell us what to do, how to proceed, we are always one with God and have the light of infinite intelligence shining within us. When we feel that we have been left on our own to find our way, it is our opportunity to stand on our own as children of God. It is our opportunity to listen, really listen, to the still small voice within us that is our guide and counselor.

And I will lead the blind
in a way that they know not,
in paths that they have not known
I will guide them.
I will turn the darkness before
them into light,
the rough places into level ground.

(Isa. 42:16)

The one on a new job, the student in a new school, the one learning a new skill, all are on their own, but not alone. We are meant for success and fulfillment. God's light is with us to show us the way.

When illness strikes, a person may be surrounded by loving family and friends, he may have excellent care and medical attention, but still feel very much alone and on his own in his need. We are never alone in any time of need, for God is with us. God helps us to be on our own even when the need is for healing.

What does it mean to be on our own when we are praying to be healed? It means to realize that our healing is not dependent on someone or something outside ourselves. It means to realize that healing comes from within us, that the capacity for renewal and restoration is built into our very body structure, that life and health are the natural pattern and response of the cells that make up our bodies. To be on our own is to know that our bodies are the temple of the living God, that we are meant for life and perfection. When we can stand on our own in knowing the truth about ourselves, we hasten the healing processes. We can stand on our own spiritually, for we do not stand alone. We are strengthened and empowered by the living Spirit within us.

With the loss of a husband or a wife, a person may cry out: "How can I go on? How can I cope with life?" He or she may not be able to see how life can be bearable without the love and support and companionship of a dear one. It is not easy to face the changes that bereavement brings. Where there has been a sharing of daily life, now the bereaved are on their own. On their own, but not alone.

The need for strength, for courage, for comfort is met by the loving presence of Christ in our midst. *"Peace I leave with you; my peace I give to you; not as the world gives do I give to you. Let not your hearts be troubled, neither let them be afraid"* (John 14:27). *"Lo, I am with you always."*

Always the loving Christ Spirit is with us, supporting us, bringing us peace, renewing us in courage, and giving us the will to carry on.

We can cope; we can meet life in a new spirit; we can rely on the loving Christ Spirit within us to heal the hurts of the heart and to bring us into newness of joy. We are on our own, but we are not alone.

No one tells the baby struggling to stand, trying to manage that first step, that he is on his own. He knows it; it is his first move toward independence. His parents, as much as they love him, as much as they want to help him in every way, cannot do for him what he must do for himself. They can encourage him, praise him, rejoice in his progress; but he must learn to stand on his own. He must take that first step on his own. He is on his own, but not alone, for even the tiny infant has within him the Spirit of God that is his inner support, his inner strength, his inner power to be and to become.

Sometimes we may feel like an infant struggling to get to our feet, trying to take the needed step that will take us out of weakness and dependency into a new and rewarding and fulfilling way of life.

A friend said that she was crushed when her husband of thirty years wanted a divorce. Weeks and months after the divorce she still refused to accept it, still refused to give him up. But she said that she kept trying to know the truth, trying to see the good in the experience. Suddenly she made up her mind to help herself and then, she said, change began to take place. She says that she has come from darkness into light, and that God has blessed her beyond words. For the first time in her life she is really learning and growing. She says that she now understands what people mean when they say that even though outer conditions in their lives have not changed, something within has changed. This friend is finding a new life. She is beginning to learn how to live on her own. She knows that she is on her own, but not alone, for God is with her.

All of us want to be strong. We want to be able to stand on our own two feet. We want to be able to cope with life, to be free from fear and dependency. But none of us wants to be alone. We find that we are not alone, ever, in any experience, in any situation, at any time. Always God is with us, for God is the very life in which we live. *"In him we live and move and have our being"* (Acts 17:28). God's Spirit in us calls us to come up higher in our thought about ourselves. God's Spirit in us gives us the strength, the courage, the will, the faith to refuse to be downed by circumstances. God's Spirit in us helps us to stand strong, to be on our own.

We are on our own, but we are not alone, for God is with us.

You Can Afford the Pearl
of Great Price

Can you afford it? I'm not talking about money or about things you may or may not think you can afford. I'm talking about feelings and thoughts and attitudes that you definitely cannot afford.

A friend was telling me recently how hurt and upset she was by the way another friend had treated her. She said, "It's all I can think about. It's actually making me ill." She really can't afford to continue in this vein of thought. The cost is too great. No matter how justified she feels in her reactions to her friends's disloyalty, she cannot afford to continue to harbor hurt feelings.

We have it in our power to change our feelings, but it is not always easy to do so. We have to take command, to decide that we will no longer continue in unhappy states of mind. What we want is the "pearl of great price" which we can afford. The pearl of great price is faith, trust, the inner knowing that we are one with God.

All of us have our dreams, our goals, our desires, and we must be willing to make the effort, pay the price, to achieve their fulfillment.

As we think about our lives and the ways in which we would make them better, let us determine not to carry along beliefs, feelings, or attitudes that we can't afford, that hamper our growth, that separate us in thought from God, that keep us from being and expressing all that we know we can be and express.

Unforgiveness? We can't afford it!

If we have held ourselves or anyone else in a thought of unforgiveness, if we keep remembering some happening of the past with remorse and self-condemnation, or if we cannot forgive another for something he or she did or said, it's time to forgive ourselves, it's time to forgive others. It's time to accept

the forgiving love of Christ so that even the
memory of something we thought we could
never forgive is as waters that have passed
away. We accept the pearl of great price that
we can afford—forgiving love—and we are at
peace.

Hurt feelings, resentment, self-pity. We
can't afford them!

We can't afford hurt feelings, resentment,
self-pity, but we can afford the pearl of great
price, which in this instance is a new self-
image. We are easily hurt and put on the de-
fensive when we do not accept ourselves and
our worth, when we do not have a clear realization of who and what we are. We are spiritual beings. In our divine self we are wonderful, capable. In our divine self we are secure.
In our divine self we are loved and we are loving. In our divine self we are God's image.

We cannot afford and do not want to continue in thoughts and feelings that make us
feel small and weak. We want and can afford
the pearl of great price—the knowledge of our
divine self—that calls us to greatness of
spirit, that inspires us to express the Christ
qualities that make life joyous and fulfilling.

To dwell on our aches and pains, to think of ourselves as weak or old—we can't afford it!

We can't afford to identify with illness, lack of life or strength. We can't afford to magnify symptoms. We can't afford to think of ourselves as old or decrepit. How we see ourselves, what we tell ourselves about our health or lack of health has a definite effect on us. We can afford the pearl of great price, which is the realization that we are truly wonderfully made, that our bodies are the temples of the living God, that their trillions of cells were created out of the very life of God. The pearl of great price that we can afford is the realization and the faith that we are meant to be well, strong, healthy, radiantly alive. No matter what the appearance, all can be healed, for God is our life and that life is eternal, abiding.

To give way to our fears, to give up on life? We can't afford it!

We can't afford to let fear be our first reaction to the happenings in our lives or in the lives of our dear ones. We can't afford to be fearful concerning our prosperity and well-being and the prosperity and well-being of our dear ones. We can't afford to be fearful of the future, to project negative thoughts, to let our imagination paint a dark picture.

What we can afford—the pearl of great price—is trust, trust in God, trust in ourselves, trust in God's Spirit within us, trust in God's Spirit within our dear ones. The pearl of great price that we can afford is trust in the outworking of good in all that concerns us, trust that in the circumstances and conditions that seem difficult, God is there, God is at work, good is being brought forth.

The pearl of great price that we can afford is trust in the flowing quality of life, ever upward, ever working toward the ultimate good.

I Am the Way

There is a way to solve the problem that we cannot seem to solve. There is a way to meet that need which is a source of worry and anxiety to us. We may have been affirming that there is a way. We may have been praying, "God, show me the way." Now let us make a leap in faith and know: *I am the way.*

When Jesus said: *"I am the way, and the truth, and the life"* (John 14:6), He was giving us a most important key to overcoming. Are we searching for a way? The way is in us. God in us, the Christ self in us, says, "I am the way."

The way of the I AM, the Christ in us, is the way of light, the way of wisdom. When we affirm *I am the way,* even though there seems to be no way, light dawns in the darkness, clouds lift, answers seem suddenly to appear. The way opens, the solution is shown, not in some mysterious happening but in natural and logical turns of events.

When we begin with inner faith in the Christ in us as the way, outer help, outer guides, outer avenues appear. A way opens up. With Christ there is always a way. And where is Christ? In our midst, assuring us, "I am the way."

Are we unhappy? *I am the way of happiness.* This is true, for our happiness cannot be given to us by another, cannot come from another. Another person may add to our happiness, but happiness begins within us.

If we long for more happiness in our lives, more love, more joy, let us make the leap in faith and affirm: *I am the way of happiness.* We may have been praying, "God, show me the way to be happy." We may have been praying to know how to change our lives. We may have been praying for people to be drawn to us who will enrich our lives and add joy to our living. But the beginning is in us.

I am the way of happiness. I AM, the Christ in us, is love, peace, joy, understanding, is all that we long to be and to express.

There is a way to have a happier life. There is a way to have rewarding, enriching experiences. There is a way to have cherished relationships. *I am the way.* As we let Christ come forth in us, we do not have to plan the way. The way will open up; people will appear; conditions will change. We shall be happy, not because of these things but because we are expressing the happy Self that we are essentially.

If the way to healing has been a long journey, or if healing seems to have been blocked by some appearance, some condition, here, too, let us make our leap in faith and declare: *I am health; I am life.* Where we have prayed to be shown the way to overcome fear and belief in disease, now let us know that we are one with life itself. There is nothing to fear. *"I am the way, and the truth, and the life."*

The life of Christ is in us. The substance of our bodies is composed of Christ-life. The cells of our bodies respond to the call of life. If some outer help or treatment is needed, the way will be shown to us. If there are attitudes or feelings of anxiety and fear standing in the way of healing, we will be shown how to overcome them. But these things are not the healing. They add to the healing, but Christ in us is the life, the healing.

I am the Christ. I am that in you which is deathless, ageless, indomitable, undefeatable. I am that in you which is far beyond anything you have believed yourself to be. Trust Me. I am the way. I am the Christ in you.

Right Now the Resurrection

Resurrection is not a word that we usually think of in relation to our own life, as something we have experienced and are experiencing now. But we have all experienced resurrection, and are experiencing it now, though we may call it by another name.

We have all known someone who, when hopes and dreams seemed shattered, has had the courage and the faith to make a new start, a new beginning. That was resurrection!

There is a resurrecting spirit in us, a spirit that enables us to begin again, to overcome limitations, to change our thinking and our life. But we must want to; we must have the motivation, the incentive to rise up from the dead, as it were, to come to life, to let the energy and life of the Christ impel us forward.

When we make up our mind that we are no longer going to stay down in the depths of defeat or despair, it seems as though the powers of the universe rush to our aid, as though God takes our hand and lifts us up.

Resurrected? Of course, you have been!

That time when you felt down in spirit, disheartened about yourself and your affairs, and then someone or something changed the trend of your thinking, reminded you of your ability to cope with life, gave you a lift, set your heart singing—that was a resurrection!

Resurrected? Of course you are being resurrected!

Every time you are able to forgive and forget some injury or hurt, every time you are able to bless and behold the Christ in another, that is a resurrection—a resurrection into the larger love of God, a resurrection into the forgiving love of Jesus Christ.

Every time you affirm life and health and wholeness and your body responds by showing forth the strength and perfection that is its natural state, that is a resurrection. You are resurrected into the realization of the eternal life of God—ever-renewing, ever-unfolding, ever-perfecting and healing your body temple.

Every time you gain dominion and mastery over fearful thoughts and feelings, every time you prove that you are not at the mercy of your moods, that you are stronger than any limiting thought or habit, that is a resurrection—a resurrection into the perfect freedom of spirit that is yours as a child of God, the freedom of Christ in you.

Every time you know the truth about yourself, the truth that you are more than flesh and blood, that you are a spiritual being with divine powers and capabilities—that is a resurrection, a resurrection into a new way of thinking and living.

We enter into the living consciousness of Jesus Christ as we incorporate His words into our consciousness. It is good to think of Jesus' words: *"I am the resurrection and the life"* (John 11:25), to affirm them, to follow Jesus in this marvelous affirmation of life.

What are we saying when we say, "I am the resurrection and the life"? We are identifying with the lifting power of the Christ, with the eternal life of the Christ. We may have thought, "Someday I will be resurrected; someday I will have eternal life." But to follow Jesus is to affirm: *I am the resurrection and the life.* This is an affirmation of life, not of the future but of the here and now.

Charles Fillmore says: *Right now the resurrection work is going on, and men and women are awakening to a new consciousness of life, understanding, and bodily perfection.*

Right now the resurrection work is going on in you.

Right now you are being resurrected into newness of life.

Right now you are rising to a new and higher place in consciousness.

Right now your spirit is being lifted up, your faith is being strengthened.

Right now the morning of Truth dawns in your soul.

Make a Prosperity Breakthrough

Just as a healing breakthrough comes when connection is made with the life source, so a prosperity breakthrough is made when we make connection with the one source, the substance underlying all manifestation.

The connecting link between us and God is our mind. The flow of prosperity starts from within us; it has its beginning in ideas. Just as a mighty river at its source may be a small stream, so the mighty river of the substance of God begins its flow as a small stream of rich ideas, flowing to us, through us, from the Mind of God.

What is a rich idea? It is any idea that engenders increase, that produces conditions of well-being, any idea that brings prosperity to us and others. No one ever proved the law of prosperity without first having an idea—an idea that evolved within, an idea that he or she acted upon to change conditions, to create a new climate in which riches—inner and outer—could grow and flourish.

A prospering idea is needed when there is lack of any kind. If we need a job, we may be doing a great deal of thinking about it. We may be pursuing every avenue that might lead to work. We may be praying, perhaps desperately, for a job. But we may not have a prosperity thought, a divine idea, about ourselves or our prospects of finding our right place.

I am talented. I am able. I am a needed part of God's creation. The divine idea we need in order to find employment may be the realization that even more than we need a job, there is a job that needs us. The good we seek is seeking us. The supply is there before the demand is made upon it. The right job is there. We make connection with it by affirming our oneness with it, by knowing that we have something to give, that we are needed.

A friend said recently, "I have found a job, praise the Lord! It is different from anything I have ever done before, but it is a wonderful answer to my prayer." She found a job, and a job found her. She made her prosperity breakthrough, made connection with the divine source, and the need of a job was supplied.

Recession, depression, inflation—how can we cope with them? These are man-made conditions and cannot affect the underlying truth of God's substance, God's all-providing supply and support. In the midst of changing times and conditions, we can maintain a sense of security. We can feel prosperous. We can demonstrate supply for our needs. We can refuse to let fear color our thinking and cloud our world.

If we are in some sort of financial strait and it seems as though there is no way for us to meet our obligations or hold out against financial disaster, let us pray that our faith holds out. The money need will take care of itself if the needed faith is there.

Jesus said: *"Do not be anxious about your life, what you shall eat, nor about your body, what you shall put on"* (Luke 12:22). *"Your*

Father knows that you need them. Instead, seek his kingdom, and these things shall be yours as well" (John 12:30, 31). He also said: *"Fear not, little flock, for it is your Father's good pleasure to give you the kingdom"* (Luke 12:32).

The right job, the right home, the money with which to meet monthly bills—we have every reason to expect such needs to be met. There is no virtue in being poor, in being without the necessities of life. We are children of a rich God. We were born to be rich. More than just money in the bank or stocks and bonds, prosperity is a way of thought, a way of life. It includes well-being, a sense of being needed, a feeling of fulfillment and satisfaction.

Prosperity is not the result of praying to get something. It is the result of fulfilling the law of giving and receiving. This balance is necessary to the achievement of true prosperity.

We each have something to give—actually much to give. We have talents, latent perhaps, buried perhaps. We can give of them only as we call them forth and use them. We have abilities that are needed, that can add something constructive and helpful to our world. We have love that when expressed can be the ultimate gift, the gift that transforms and blesses all it touches. But we have to give of what we have.

The idea of giving and receiving is a divine idea that helps us make connection with the underlying substance, ever-flowing from the Fountainhead, the Source. It is a divine idea that keeps the connection unbroken.

If you need prosperity, ask yourself, "What do I have to give?" Pray to be shown how to give, what to give, how to serve. Your prospering idea will come through you. You will enlarge and increase the scope of your life and its interests and activities.

"The measure you give will be the measure you get" (Matt. 7:2).

A prospering idea that many of us need to lay hold of is the faith to know that not only will today's needs be met but that future needs will be met as well. Many people think too much in terms of future lack. They prepare for it in thought, and they prepare for it in outer ways. It is good to have savings, pension plans, and so on, but it is not good to place our sole dependence in such things and feel uneasy and fearful as to what changing conditions may do to our future security.

Jesus said: *"Where your treasure is, there will your heart be also"* (Matt. 6:21). Are we giving our heart, that is, our feeling, our emotional support, to something we look to as our supply?

Our treasure is our feeling of spiritual security. Our treasure is knowing that we are a child of God, a spiritual being. Our treasure is knowing that we are always one with God, our Source, and that in God and through God our needs are met, constantly, abundantly, on time, unfailingly. Our treasure is our realization of the enduring things of the Spirit— life, love, joy, peace, faith.

Prosperity breakthrough? You can make it! It does not matter how long you have lived with the poverty idea. You can be freed from it. You can be healed of lack and limitation.

Do you feel guilty about praying for prosperity? Why should you? Jesus said: *"Ask, and it will be given you; seek, and you will find; knock, and it will be opened to you. For every one who asks receives, and he who seeks finds, and to him who knocks it will be opened. Or what man of you, if his son asks him for bread, will give him a stone? Or if he asks for a fish, will give him a serpent? If you then... know how to give good gifts to your children, how much more will your Father who is in heaven give good things to those who ask him!"* (Matt. 7:7-11)

Make your prosperity breakthrough by putting behind you old beliefs in lack and limitation, old beliefs that somehow you are not worthy of prosperity or success, old beliefs that you have nothing to give, nothing to offer to life or to others.

Make your prosperity breakthrough. Make connection with your source by turning to God in prayer and meditation, by affirming your oneness with God, the Source.

Make your prosperity breakthrough. Affirm your spiritual status. Affirm: *I am a radiant, all-wise, all-loving, all-conquering child of God. Infinite wisdom guides me, divine love prospers me, and I am successful in all that I undertake.* Affirm this and believe this, for it is the truth about you.

Open your mind to prospering ideas and then use the ideas that come. Put them to work! Do not reject an idea that comes to you because it does not seem unusual or out of the ordinary. It may be the right idea, the idea that can form the basis for growth and unfoldment and success.

Think of a prospering idea as a seed. A seed may look small, insignificant, even lifeless, but it has the potential, when nurtured, to produce results. You nurture prosperity ideas through your prayers and faith, through your interest and enthusiasm, through your persistence in practicing the principle of giving and receiving.

You are needed and important. You are a beloved child of God. You are now and forever one with God, the unfailing, everlasting Source and supplier of all substance.

Make your prosperity breakthrough. Prove the law for yourself.

Make a Healing Breakthrough

A friend asked, "Do I have to be perfect to be healed?"

Healing is not a matter of reward and punishment. It is a matter of connecting with the powerful life-force within us. We may short-circuit this connection by giving way to fear and anxiety, by dwelling on thoughts of resentment, unforgiveness, bitterness. But always the life is there within us; always we can make the healing breakthrough.

For example, it is not a matter of reward or punishment when electric current needs to be restored. We have to put the plug in the socket in order to make the connection, and the connection has to remain unbroken in order that the current may flow.

God does not say, "You must be perfect before you can be healed." God says: *Because I have created you perfect, you can be healed.*

Jesus said to the man by the pool, who had been ill for 38 years: *"Do you want to be healed?"* The man who had been hoping for some kind of miracle healing from the waters of the pool said that he had no one to lower him into the pool. Jesus said: *"Take up your pallet, and walk."* The connection was made, the healing breakthrough came. *And at once the man was healed, and he took up his pallet and walked* (John 5:6, 8, 9). Not in the waters in the pool but within him was the healing life and power.

Healing is of the whole person, but healing of the body is not deferred until every thought is perfect, until every word is wise, until every part of life is in order and harmony. Very few healings would take place were this the case.

Jesus was very compassionate, yet never faltered in proclaiming life, no matter what the condition or how long its duration. He helped those in need of healing to make connection with the life-force within them, to make a healing breakthrough. He saw them whole; He saw them perfect. He said: *"Your faith has made you well"* (Matt. 9:22). He spoke the word of healing and, for many who heard, there was an instant response. They felt a renewal of life. Mind, body, and soul felt the healing current. They literally came to life.

Silent Unity follows Jesus in proclaiming life, in reminding all who ask for healing prayers that the powerful life of God is within them. We say, "You can be healed." We pray for healing and we hold to our vision of the perfect self, the Christ self, in all for whom we pray. We remind them that they are meant to be healthy, vitally alive, that they are meant to be loving, joyous, creative. We know that there is, innate in everyone, a longing for Truth, a longing for light, a longing to be more than they have yet expressed.

I think this is why the prayers of Silent Unity are so effective, for they are felt as a great outpouring of love and life by those who have been tempted to give up, to accept illness and unhappiness as their lot, who may have been berating themselves for their failures, who may feel unworthy or wonder where they have gone wrong.

Jesus healed the sick, but more than that He gave a message of life—eternal life. He said: *"Your sins are forgiven"* (Matt. 9:2). What sins? The sins of negative thoughts and feelings, false beliefs that keep us bound to sickness and disease, to unhappiness, to all the limitations of mortal mind.

The healthiest people probably think the least about health as such, but they are health-minded, they are life-minded.

Health, true health, is health of mind, health of body, health of soul. Health is of the whole person.

The evidence is all on the side of life. That we are meant to live vitally, healthily, with energy and enthusiasm is the basis for all healing. That there is a relation between our thoughts and attitudes and our state of health is being accepted by more and more people.

Jesus Christ brought a message of life to the world. His words were life-giving. He healed those who turned to Him. He did not

ask, "Are you worthy of healing?" He did not
say, "This condition is incurable." He did not
say, "You'll just have to live with this
chronic complaint." Someone has rightly said
that Jesus had no "patients." He healed, and
the sick took up their beds; that is, they went
about the business of living. When He healed
Peter's mother-in-law, she rose and prepared
dinner.

In an article in "Reader's Digest," Lewis
Thomas, chancellor of the world's largest can-
cer research center in New York, was quoted
as saying: *"I believe fervently in our species
and have no patience with the current fashion
of running down the human being ... On the
contrary, we are a spectacular, splendid manifestation of life. We matter. We are the
newest, youngest, brightest thing around."*

The article says that Dr. Thomas believes
that our exaggerated fear of germs is related
to our constant uneasiness about health, that
for many people the presence of good health
is something only reluctantly acknowledged,
as if it might be snatched away at any time.
Yet in real life, he insists, *we are amazingly
tough and durable ... You'd think that the*

mere fact of existing would keep us all in a contented dazzlement. You'd think we'd never stop dancing.

Charles Fillmore, co-founder of Unity, had a marvelously vital concept of life, a concept that he proved for himself. He was still dancing for joy in the thought of life when at age 94 he wrote this affirmation: *I fairly sizzle with zeal and enthusiasm and spring forth with a mighty faith to do the things that ought to be done by me.*

In the 15th chapter of I Corinthians we read: *There are celestial bodies and there are terrestrial bodies . . . If there is a physical body, there is also a spiritual body. Thus it is written, "The first man Adam became a living being"; the last Adam became a life-giving spirit . . . For this perishable nature must put on the imperishable, and this mortal nature must put on immortality. When the perishable puts on the imperishable, and the mortal puts on immortality, then shall come to pass the saying that is written: "Death is swallowed up in victory."*

The Christ in us is the "last Adam," which is a life-giving Spirit. Are we seeking life and health? We have a life-giving Spirit in us! As the Christ of God in expression, we become a life-giving spirit. This realization gives new meaning to many of the words of life that we may not have thought of as relating to us, to our own health and well-being.

Charles Fillmore says: *When man realizes that "death and life are in the power of the tongue" and begins to use his "I am" statements wisely, he has the key that unlocks the secret chambers of existence in heaven and earth.*

The highest "I am" statements are the words of Jesus. Jesus said that we are to keep His words. The way to keep His words is to make them our own, to identify with them, to affirm them, to live with them.

Think of some of the words of Jesus that are powerful "I am" statements.

"I am the way, and the truth, and the life" (John 14:6).

"I am the light of the world" (John 8:12).

"Before Abraham was, I am" (John 8:58).

"I am the bread of life" (John 6:35).

"I am the resurrection and the life" (John 11:25).

When we make these powerful "I am" statements, we are speaking them in the name of Jesus Christ, the Son in us, in whom we have life.

This is the testimony, that God gave us eternal life, and this life is in his Son. He who has the Son has life (I John 5:11, 12).

The Christ in us is the second Adam, the Son of God. In the Son, the Christ of our being, we have eternal life.

Make this your affirmation: *I am eternally alive through the life of Christ in me, the life-giving Spirit of my being.*

Do you not know that your body is a temple of the Holy Spirit within you, which you have from God? . . . So glorify God in your body (I Cor. 6:19, 20). Your body is the temple of God, and you are the life-giving Spirit that dwells in that temple. To glorify God in your body is to show forth the life of God, to express life, vitality, and energy.

"I came that they may have life, and have it abundantly" (John 10:10). Think about these words of Jesus and affirm that Christ, the life-giving Spirit, has come into your consciousness, bringing health and renewal.

Affirm: *In Christ I am a life-giving Spirit. In Christ I am wholly and vitally alive.*

I am the bread of life. Make this word of Jesus Christ your own word. What is the bread of life? It is the substance of life, the essence of life, the life-force. Think of your body as composed of the very substance of God-life, as being in truth the "bread of life." Make this your affirmation: *I am the bread of life. I am fed and nourished and rejuvenated by the living bread.*

"As Moses lifted up the serpent in the wilderness, so must the Son of man be lifted up, that whoever believes in him may have eternal life" (John 3:14, 15). When we lift up our consciousness to the Christ, we enter the living Christ consciousness, the consciousness of eternal life. *"For this is the will of my Father, that every one who sees the Son and believes in him should have eternal life"* (John 6:40).

"I am the resurrection and the life; he who believes in me, though he die, yet shall he live, and whoever lives and believes in me shall never die" (John 11:25, 26). This is the great "I am" statement that lifts us into a new con-

sciousness of life. When we affirm: *I am the resurrection and the life,* we are entering the Christ consciousness of life. When we affirm: *I am the resurrection and the life,* our thoughts are lifted up, our feelings are lifted up, everything in us turns to the idea of life—life that is health for our bodies, life that is health for our souls, life that is health for our minds, life that is joy and happiness and a sense of well-being on every level of consciousness, in every phase of our existence.

Norman Cousins, who wrote about his healing through laughter, says: *I have learned never to underestimate the capacity of the human mind and body to regenerate—even when the prospects seem most wretched. The life-force may be the least understood force on earth.*

Cousins also says: *Long before my own serious illness, I became convinced that creativity, the will to live, hope, faith, and love have biochemical significance and contribute strongly to healing and to well-being. The positive emotions are life-giving experiences.*

When you feel weak or ill, regenerate your will to live, reaffirm your faith. Make your own healing breakthrough; have your own life-giving experience. It is possible because you are a life-giving spirit. Whenever thoughts of gloom or fear or unhappiness try to enter, lift up your thoughts, lift up your faith. Make strong affirmations of life, of fearlessness, of faith, of joy. By affirming powerful, life-giving ideas, you make your own healing breakthrough, you connect with the healing current of life within you, you come to life—mind, body, and soul.

Following are some affirmations you may want to make for yourself and incorporate into your consciousness:

A perfect pattern of life is built into me.

Disease has no part of me.

The perfect body idea cannot die. I am the resurrection and the life. I am one with eternal life.

I am spirit, mind, and body—one—not separate.

The substance of my body is spiritual; I am one with God-life. Yet in my flesh shall I see God (Job. 19:26 A.V.).

Christ, the life-giving Spirit in me, gives life to my body, life to my mind, life to my spirit.

You Are a Star

Every time a child comes into the world it is as though he has been waiting in the wings ready to take his place center stage, to play his starring role in the production he will call his life.

Have you found your starring role? Or do you feel as though you are still waiting in the wings?

When Jesus came into the world, a star was born. When you came into the world, a star was born. Jesus knew His role. You may have been searching for your role, searching for your place in life, searching for purpose and meaning.

What is a star? A light giver. To fulfill your

role as a star on the stage of life, you must be a light giver.

Not everyone can be the star in a theatrical production, but everyone can be a star in his own sphere, everyone can be a light giver.

A poet has said:

Hold thy lighted lamp on high,
Be a star in someone's sky.

You may say, "I am not much; my life is not much." But you can be a star in your own life experience, and you can be a star in someone's sky by holding high your lamp of faith.

You may feel that your light is more like a tiny candle than a star. But it has been truly said that no darkness in the world can put out the light of one small candle. You can be a light, a little light perhaps, but still a light that shines in the dark. And one small candle can light other candles without losing any of its own light.

This is *the mystery hidden for ages and generations . . . Christ in you, the hope of glory* (Col. 1:26, 27). To realize this is to find the answer to our search for meaning and purpose in life. To know that Christ is in us, our hope of glory, is to know that our desire to be more, to express more, is not a vain dream but spiritual intuition.

Christ in us is our hope of glory, the fulfillment of our true destiny. When we realize that Christ is in us, we are reborn into a new realization of who we are and why we are. If Christ is in us, our hope of glory, if we are expressions of Christ in the world, our purpose and our role are clear. We are to express the Christ, to bring Christ into the world of thought, the world of action, the world around us.

Christ is light; we are to express the Christ light, to let it shine through us. Let us light the candle of faith. Let us be stars of light in our world, stars in someone's sky.

Christ is peace; we are to express peace, to bring peace to our own minds and hearts, to give our peace to others.

Christ is love; we are to express love. Our purpose, our starring role in life, is to truly love the people in our lives, to look past differences, to be blind to faults, to love with Christlike love—the love that sees the inner perfection and Godlikeness in all.

Christ is life. We are to express life, to radi-

ate a spirit of wholeness and well-being, to be
vital and enthusiastic. We express life as we
pray for healing, as we have faith in God's
power to heal those for whom we pray. We
fulfill our starring role as we keep faith in life
and remember that we live in eternity now.

Lift Your Vision

Some impressions stay with us always. In my mind's eye I can still see May Rowland, who was the director of Silent Unity for more than fifty years and one of the great spiritual leaders in Unity, standing poised and serene, talking with a woman who was crying and most distraught. I thought, how can May be so calm in the face of this woman's visible agitation?

I learned from May Rowland and from my long association with Silent Unity that we help others most by standing with them in faith rather than by taking on their problems. We want to be loving and caring and sensitive to the needs of others and we want also to help them know that they have the God-given capacity to rise out of depression, to overcome grief, to meet their problems, to find a happier, better way of life.

In Silent Unity, when we pray for others, we pray first for our own illumination. We pray to increase our own faith, we pray to lift up our own thoughts, our own consciousness.

When we are concerned about others and their problems, we must remember that our first need is to pray for our own illumination.

As long as we are worried and troubled about another, we need to be lifted, our consciousness needs to be lifted. As long as we see only another's needs and problems, we have a problem, too. We need to lift our vision, to see beyond the needs and problems to the Spirit of God in that one. We need to hold to the truth that all can be changed, that with God all things are possible. As long as we are fearful about another's state of health, we, too, are in need of a healing consciousness. We need to lift our own thoughts, to hold to the life idea, to have faith in the healing Christ to restore and to make whole. As long as we spend sleepless nights worrying about our dear ones, their problems are our problems. We need to release our dear ones into God's care and keeping, to let go and let God, to have faith that God is with them, their help in every need.

We want to help, and we can, as we keep our faith in God strong. We help others in our prayers and in our association with them as we see not weakness but strength, as we see not despair but faith and confidence, as we say to one who says, "I can't! It's impossible!" "You can! With God all things are possible!"

Perhaps what others want most from us is the feeling and the faith that there is a way to meet and overcome their problems. They would say to us, "Don't let me down. Be strong. Don't make me feel less than I am. Tell me of my strength. Encourage me to believe in God, to believe in myself. Encourage me to stand on my own two feet."

If you are concerned about someone, pray for that one, of course, but first of all pray to be lifted in faith, to be filled with the strong assurance of God's presence and power, never-failing, at work in you and in your dear one now. Above all, pray that you may be a blessing, that you may serve as a channel through which God's work is done.

The Answer Is Always Yes

Many people have said many things about prayer. But the best way to define prayer is to practice it, to experience it.

Most of us know more about prayer than we think we do; we pray more often, more effectively than we realize. It has been said:

Prayer is the soul's sincere desire,
Uttered or unexpressed.

Conscious, positive, constructive thinking is a kind of prayer. Unconscious thought is a kind of prayer. Reactions and feelings, are a kind of prayer. Our inner conversation with ourselves is a kind of prayer.

We hear much about the value of meditation as a way of prayer. If God is within us, then the place to find God is in the stillness of our own being. Meditation helps us to center our thoughts in God, to attune our hearts to God, to focus our whole attention on the presence of God in our midst. Meditation is sometimes called the "silence." In the silence of our soul, which is reached by way of meditation, we feel our oneness with God, with all that God is. We are in the presence of pure Being, in the presence of love, life, peace, power, wisdom, and joy. Beyond thought, beyond words, we feel and know that God is and we are. There is power in the silence. From the soundless depths of being power flows. We connect with this power in the place of stillness within us, the secret place, the place we come to when we say to self, to thoughts, to feelings, to emotions: *"Be still, and know that I am God"* (Psalms 46:10).

Thinking is a kind of prayer, but not all kinds of thoughts are prayers. The kind of thinking that gives us self-confidence and inspires us to constructive, positive action, this is prayer. The kind of thinking that gives us insight and understanding of ourselves and others, this is prayer. The kind of thinking that refuses to accept negative opinions, that searches for Truth and light, this is prayer.

Thinking is a kind of prayer that changes our life; thinking is conscious prayer in action.

It has been said that prayer changes things. The thinking kind of prayer changes lives. *For as he* (man) *thinketh in his heart, so is he* (Prov. 23:7 A.V.). Heart-thinking is a kind of prayer that spiritualizes our attitudes and approach to life. It is a kind of thinking that we are capable of as spiritual beings, endowed with God's own Spirit.

When we have a problem, we are told that we should think about God and not the problem. This is often easier said than done. We may be consumed with the thought of the problem. We may spend sleepless nights wondering how we are to solve it. It is *our* problem, we feel. We cannot expect God to solve it for us, we tell ourselves.

The answer is there, of course, the solution is at hand, but we need to open ourselves to light, to make of ourselves channels through which wisdom and intelligence can flow. Stewing and fretting and trying to think our way through a problem is not prayer. The kind of prayer needed is to let go and let God take over, to think about God, the unfailing power for good at work in us and in all that concerns us. Just the words *God is here; God is in charge* may be all that we need to hold to in order for us to release the problem and rest in faith and trust. Light will come, answers will come, we will see our way clearly. The answer is always yes.

For the Son of God, Jesus Christ . . . was not Yes and No; but in him it is always Yes. For all the promises of God find their Yes in him (II Cor. 1:19, 20).

All the promises of God find their yes in Christ, the Spirit of God in us. To know this is to know where human power ends and divine power begins. This is what it means to think about God instead of thinking about the problem. There is a divinity within us, the Christ self, that gives us yes answers to our seeking, that makes us know we have within us spiritual powers and capabilities, spiritual greatness. How small our human problems seem, how easily they are solved, as we take them to God in prayer, as we release them and let our whole being enter a time of praise and rejoicing for the wonderful power at work in us and in our lives. The answer is always yes!

When we take a small step in prayer, we can expect large results. The power of prayer is a multiplying power, for the power behind prayer is faith. Jesus spoke of the multiplying power of faith. He likened it to a grain of mustard seed. Prayer that is a prayer of faith, faith that says, "I believe," and really means it, can work miracles. Jesus said: *"Whoever says to this mountain, 'Be taken up and cast into the sea,' and does not doubt in his heart . . . will be done for him"* (Mark 11:23). Here again is the heart-prayer. The prayer that we make from our hearts, in faith removes mountains of care, brings forth miracles of health and help of every kind.

Prayer is more than just a time set aside to commune with God, although it is important that we set aside time daily for quiet prayer and meditation. Prayer is continuous. We are told that we should pray without ceasing. We are praying without ceasing as we keep ourselves centered in the truth wherever we are, whatever we are doing. We may be very active and involved with the affairs of our world, but behind the scenes, in our inner realm of thought, in our heart of hearts, we hold to our vision of Truth, we keep our minds stayed on God and God's goodness.

There are all kinds of prayers, for there are all kinds of needs. Sometimes our prayer is for strength. We need strength of will, strength of spirit, strength of determination, strength to act, to do what needs to be done, strength to carry on.

At other times our prayer is a prayer of surrender, surrender to the Most High, surrender of our will to the perfect will of God. Our need is to surrender the feeling that we must do it all, that the responsibility rests with us alone. It is a time to let go and let God take over. And in surrendering the human striving and struggling, we find that we have strength, spiritual strength.

There are prayers of denial and affirmation, but even the prayer of denial is a prayer of affirmation, for a true denial is a positive rejection of all that is negative or false or unlike God's goodness. A denial really is our denial of our belief in something less than good, our belief that evil has any power. Affirmation always follows denial.

The affirmative prayer is the yes prayer, our affirmations are our way of saying yes to the truth. Our affirmations of health say yes to life; our affirmations of harmony say yes to peace; our affirmations of wisdom say yes to light. Our affirmative prayers are prayers that put our faith into words, our assurance into words. We do not affirm the good to make it true; we affirm it because it is true.

Prayer is a way of life; prayer is life. We pray consciously; we pray unconsciously. But the more we know about prayer and the more we practice it, the more meaningful life becomes. We find that our first reaction to everything in life becomes a positive one, a Truth-based reaction. We become stronger, wiser, more loving, more understanding. We are able to meet our experiences courageously and with a spirit of faith.

There are all kinds of prayers. There are times when we pray for things. It is not wrong to pray for things, to pray specifically at times. It is how we pray, why we pray,

what the things mean to us that is important.
When we put God first, we do not seek things
for their own sake, neither do we think that it
is a virtue to be poor and in want, or to be sick
and in pain.

The highest form of prayer is the prayer
that does not ask for anything, the prayer
that is a great and glorious "Thank You,
God!" The prayer of thanksgiving is truly a
prayer of faith. It voices our thanks before a
need is met. It says with Jesus: *"Father, I
thank thee that thou hast heard me. I knew
that thou hearest me always"* (John 11:41,
42). The prayer of thanks rises to our lips, fills
our hearts and minds because we know and
believe that in God, in Christ, the answer is
always yes!

You Are Secure in God

What is security? Is it the feeling that goes with a steady job, a regular income, an expectation of enough to live on in future days? It is true that this is part of what goes to make up a sense of security. However, if every employed person in the world were guaranteed his present job and salary for the rest of his life, he would still be far from having security in its truest meaning.

Why? Because security does not come from without but from within. Security springs from an inner assurance of mind and heart and soul. It is the sustained realization of God's presence and power that lifts one above fear and defeat, unhappiness, or discouragement. Security feeds on the well-spring of faith and joy within and keeps one confident, optimistic, and unafraid. It is the reward of abilities and talents well used, of busy hands, of a happy heart, of a nourished soul.

Young people or people past the age that the world calls young who seek their place in life need have no fear for the future if they can learn first of all not to depend upon a job but upon God within themselves.

Today, as always since the beginning of time, there are those who see only bleak prospects, who predict a future without promise of success or achievement.

We cannot look to an institution, an industry, or the government to guarantee us security and a good living. Disappointment is sure to follow such misplaced trust. But within us is the Spirit of God that can be depended upon to guide us safely into ways of happy and successful living. The surest guarantee of security in the future is the present realization of the help and inspiration of God within. *"God shows no partiality, but in every nation any one who fears him and does what is right is acceptable to him"* (Acts 10:34, 35).

What a person works for is surely important. *"Do not labor for the food which perishes, but for the food which endures to eternal life"* (John 6:27). If we work merely for a salary we are indeed getting poor pay. For the money is soon spent and we have nothing to look forward to but another check. But if we can like our work, if we can find mental, physical, and spiritual exhilaration in doing it, then the salary is secondary and the inner reward far exceeds the money that we receive.

"Seek first his kingdom and his righteousness, and all these things shall be yours as well" (Matt. 6:33). Seek to give expression to the highest and best that is in you whatever you are doing, and you need not worry about monetary remuneration. It will take care of itself and it will more than take care of your needs.

What we need to realize is that each of us can be a success in his own way. All of us cannot expect to do the same kind of work, to fill the same job. But we all can constantly increase our particular abilities and talents and make the best possible use of them in whatever we are doing. The joy of success, after all, lies in the effort to better our past efforts, to use our brains and hands more effectively in the work that is ours.

You are a success if you are doing the task at hand to the best of your ability. You are a success if you are constantly growing in understanding, if you are making better use of your talent and creative power. You are a success if you have found God within yourself, for you have the guarantee of security that nothing and no one can take from you, come what may!

Springtime in Your Heart

Can this be the tree that stood black and bare against the winter sky, this tree of leaves, this splendid thing? Can this be the same gray, winter world, this world before us now, burgeoning with beauty?

We marvel at the return of spring, and an indescribable feeling of joy lifts our hearts at every sign of winter's end.

But more marvelous still is the renewal that takes place in human minds and hearts and lives, the renewal that does not wait for spring's return, the renewal that waits only on faith.

No transformed tree can compare with a transformed life. No flower of spring, pushing its way up through the snow is half so brave as a heart learning to love again. No green glade where violets grow is so exquisite as the forgiving and forgiven spirit.

We look at our own lives and we wonder, "Can this be me?" We wonder at the ways in which we have grown; we view our lives in the light of understanding; and we see how relentlessly the Spirit in us has carried us forward, sometimes in spite of ourselves. We see that the winters of our lives did not really ever hold full sway, that always, underneath it all, the renewing, life-giving Spirit of God was at work.

We look at the lives of others, and if we have eyes to see, ears to hear, and hearts to understand, we see marvelous things. We see the triumph of the Spirit in us over every conceivable kind of limitation. We see the weak become strong; we see the fearful become brave; we see the timid become confident; we see the sick become healthy; we see the poor become rich; we see the unhappy become contented; we see the lonely become part of life again; we see the bitter become mellow, the resentful become understanding, the hateful become kind and good.

How can such transformations be? How can we change from one kind of person to another? How can our lives take on new meaning and new patterns? How can our feet find new paths? How can our hearts find new happiness? How can our minds find new wisdom, new light?

It is because something in us has always been and always will be part of the perfect pattern. We do not always know it as we learn and grow, but there is a Spirit in us that is leading us Godward, Christward. The changes in our lives, in our feelings, in our attitudes that seem so miraculous are possible because we are becoming ourselves rather than because we are changing what we essentially are.

Something in every one of us knows, with a knowledge beyond dispute, that we are Spirit, that we are without beginning or end, that we cannot cease to be. We respond to Jesus' words: *"I am the resurrection and the life; he who believes in me, though he die, yet shall he live, and whoever lives and believes in me shall never die"* (John 11:25, 26), because we know they are true. The Spirit in us says: "This is true. This is true of you. This is true of all."

If you have felt downcast for any reason, if you have felt that you are a failure, if your strength has seemed to ebb, now is the time to declare over and over: *I am the resurrection, and the life.* The very atoms and cells of your body will respond to this word; it will be as though light were turned on in the city of self that is you. You will know what Jesus meant when He said: *"I am the light of the world." "You are the light of the world"* (Matt. 5:14). No tree in spring will be more green and growing than you; no soft south wind will be warmer than your heart; no world will declare the renewal of life more perfectly than will your world within!

Get Along with Others

A woman once said that she could be loving and harmonious if it were not for her family! It seems that they were always saying or doing things that upset her or made her impatient and unhappy with them and with herself.

In the matter of human relations—at home, at work, in any of our involvement with other persons—we may not find it easy to express love, to be patient, to be understanding, to allow others freedom to be themselves even though we do not approve of many of the things they say or do. It may not always be easy, but it is the way of peace and harmony.

We want to be loving and kind and understanding. We do not want to be critical of others, impatient with others, and we are not happy with ourselves when we find such feelings taking over in us.

If we are challenged by our human relations, what better time to practice expressing the Christ love!

Jesus said: *"By this all men will know that you are my disciples, if you have love for one another"* (John 13:35). Not how wise we are, not how talented we are, but how loving we are is what really matters.

We can practice expressing the Christ love every day, to the people right at hand—at the breakfast table, on the bus, at work, wherever we mingle and meet with others.

To express the Christ love is demanding in that it calls on us to express love to those who are unloving as well as to those who are loving, to those who displease us as well as to those who please us, to those who are difficult to get along with as well as to those who are harmonious and cooperative, to those whose company we find irritating as well as to those whose company we delight in, to those whose words and actions we cannot approve of as well as to those whom we look up to and admire.

One of the most helpful ideas we can hold to is simply this: *I behold the Christ in you.* This is an all-inclusive affirmation of the Christ love.

It is worth all the effort we make to express the Christ love, to be understanding, to be harmonious, to have good human relations. Others are blessed, of course, but we are the ones who are most benefited. It can change our lives.

Add Wings to Your World

Wings have always been a symbol of freedom, of the ability to soar above the world. Wings symbolize upliftment. Whatever we add wings to, we see as swift and light and free. On wings of song, we say, on wings of love, on wings of prayer.

We need to add wings to our world, to set ourselves and our lives free from bondage. When Jesus said: *"If you continue in my word, you are truly my disciples, and you will know the truth, and the truth will make you free,"* they answered him: *"We are descendants of Abraham, and have never been in bondage to any one. How is it that you say, 'You will be made free'?"* (John 8:31-33)

We look at ourselves and our lives and we
say, "I am a free person, I am not a slave.
I can do what I want to within reason, that
is, within the limits of the law of the land."
But then we may also ask ourselves, "Why
do I not feel free? Why do I feel bound and
burdened? Why do I feel at the mercy of my
thoughts and feelings? Why do I cower before the opinions of others? Why am I emo-
tionally involved in the affairs and concerns
of others so that I feel inextricably bound up
with them?"

To know the meaning of freedom, to be free
indeed, we have to change the character of
our thinking; we have to add wings to our
world. We have to break through the pattern
of thought with which we have surrounded
ourselves and get a view of a larger horizon.

Like the people who tried to analyze and
reason away Jesus' teaching, who looked at
themselves from a human sense and said in
effect, "This is what we are, this is our
heritage from our ancestors. We do not even
know what you are talking about," there are
persons today who reject the idea of a spiritual concept of themselves and the world.

They think they are looking at things logically and rationally. They say, "I am not in bondage to anyone or anything. What do you mean by freedom?"

When we add wings to our world, we are not flying away from our world, rather we are adding freedom and power to it. Real freedom comes when we add wings to our world through faith, when we know the truth, the truth that makes us free. What is the truth we are to know? Jesus said: *"So if the Son makes you free, you will be free indeed"* (John 8:36). The Son is the Christ, the spiritual self of us, the true character of our being. In this spiritual self we are free; through this spiritual self we find ourselves, we rise out of the old, limited ways into free, spiritual realms.

"And you will know the truth, and the truth will make you free." To know the truth is to be constantly aware of the presence and power of God; to know the truth is to see beyond appearances to the wholeness and perfection of God. To know the truth is to know that we are more than flesh and blood; we are spiritual beings, created in God's image and likeness, and having in us God's own Spirit,

the Christ. To know the Truth is to be free.

We know the truth as we pray, as we keep our minds stayed on true and good thoughts, as we see God and good in all the experiences of our lives. We know the truth as we affirm our spiritual nature, as we lift up our thoughts, our feelings, our emotions, as we add wings to our world through our faith in the Spirit in us.

Most of us have favorite affirmations that act as wings to our hearts, minds, and spirits. One special one is: *I am not bound in personal consciousness. I am free with the freedom of Spirit.* This helps me to rise out of the personal thoughts and feelings that bind me. It helps me to let go of the human tendency to criticize or worry or to condemn myself or another. It helps me to extricate myself from emotional involvement in a problem, my own or another's. It gives me wings to rise up to a high place in mind and heart where I can see with spiritual sight.

We are in the world, and we want to be. We want to be an active part of life. We want to feel close to other persons; we want to contribute to the well-being and happiness of others. We want to feel needed, wanted, and necessary. If we are truly honest with ourselves, we shall find that we do not want to be anyone else. We would not want any other life than our own, if it were offered to us. We do not want to retreat from life, to withdraw from life. We want to live freely, but with a sense of direction, a sense of purpose.

To be free, to know the truth, to live like children of God, we need to know ourselves. And the only way we can know ourselves is through the silence, through prayer, through stilling the personal self and letting the Christ come forth in us. Prayer adds the wings of faith to our world.

All Things Work Together
for Good

Once I was with friends, one of whom was about to pull up stakes and move thousands of miles away from what had been her home for many years, away from relatives and close friends.

One of the group asked, "Do you mean that you are going for good?" The answer was, "Of course, I am going for good!" She is going for good because this is the attitude with which she meets experiences.

I thought about this phrase "for good," which we often use with a negative connotation. Have you ever said or heard someone say about another, "I'm through with him for good!" Well, if we are going to be through with someone, put him out of our thoughts and life, we had better make it for good!

Like Jacob wrestling with the angel, we may not be able to let go the hurt feelings, the bitterness, the unforgiveness that have prompted the desire for total rejection. You remember that Jacob said to the angel: "*I will not let you go, unless you bless me*" (Gen. 32:26). So if ever we are tempted to think or say about someone, "I am through with you for good!" let us mean it as a blessing. What we are through with are unhappy feelings, unforgiving thoughts, bitter memories. We are through with these for good! This is to bless the unhappy situation, to cease wrestling with the angel, to pronounce it good.

Sometimes a person says, in a positive frame of mind, about some habit or way of life that has not been conducive to happiness and well-being, "I am through with that for good!" Usually this thought and emphasis are on the idea of overcoming, of having the strength and the will to reject negative ways of thought and action. It gives added power to his declaration of freedom from limiting habits of thinking and living when he also

emphasizes *for good!* We want to be free for
good from old limiting ways. We want a new
way of life, a new thought about ourselves, a
new realization of the spiritual self of us that
is all-conquering, triumphant, free Spirit. *I
am through with that for good!* is a positive
statement that gives us purpose and direction. We leave old ways behind and press forward to the new and good.

In little things that may seem unimportant, we put off our good, we put off our enjoyment of life. Once I complimented a friend
on her appearance and she said, "Well, I've
been saving this dress for good but decided I
should wear it." We have all known persons
who saved everything "for good." The lovely
clothes hung in the closet; the nice dishes or
silverware were never used; the parlor stood
dusted and unused. The best things were
carefully stored away "for good."

If we keep putting off our enjoyment of the
present, if we save everything for some
mythical good, we lose a great deal of enjoyment in living.

In our approach to life and living, we do not
want to think of some future time as the time

when we will be happy. We do not want to put off our good by thinking that when conditions are perfect we will enjoy life. Now, today, is the time to open up new vistas, to enjoy new experiences in living, to widen the expanse of our thought and interest.

When Joseph, who had been cruelly and unjustly treated by his brothers, had the perfect opportunity for revenge and retaliation, his words to them were: *"You meant evil against me; but God meant it for good"* (Gen. 50:20).

"God meant it for good." This is something to remember when we find it hard to see the good in some happening. The good is there, though it is not apparent at the time. Despite appearances, God means it for good, and good will be victorious.

One of the most helpful Unity affirmations for me has been: *All things are working together for my good, and I am working with them in the wisdom and the power of Spirit.* This, of course, is based on that beautiful passage in the Bible: *In everything God works for good with those who love him* (Rom. 8:28). Another Unity affirmation that stresses this same idea is: *I go to meet my good.* Like the friend who said, "Of course, I am going for good!" we can be sure that when we take this kind of attitude, when we go for good, when we expect to meet our good, we put ourselves in tune with that which is for our highest good and happiness.

In any change that we are making in our lives, in any human relationship that we are trying to resolve, in any desire for greater enjoyment of life, for freedom from lack or limitation, let us remember this phrase, "for good!" Are we going for good? Yes! Are we through with something or someone for good? Yes! Does God mean it for good? Yes! Fear not, all things do work together for good!

You Are Not at the Mercy
of Your Moods

It may seem to us that some persons are born with a good disposition, that they are naturally even-tempered. But a good disposition is also a matter of habit, the result of a continual effort to be loving, to be patient, to be kind.

It does not matter where we are in life, we are never too young or too old to begin to train ourselves in good thought habits so that we have control of our moods and emotions, so that we live peacefully and happily with ourselves and others.

How can we acquire the habit of a good disposition? We can begin right where we are today. This, our life, is really our proving

ground, it is our field of experience; it is the
school that never closes. The wonderful thing
is that in the simple everyday affairs of life
we can practice the largest ideas of which we
are aware. We can grow in spiritual stature in
the routine of every day; we can put on the
nature of Christ as we get the children ready
for school, as we make out reports at an office
desk, as we call on customers, as we talk over
the back fence with our neighbor.

How? is the question. The way is simple to
state; but it is not so simple to follow. The
way to have a good disposition is to have
good thoughts. Simple, is it not? But it takes
practice and prayer to have only good
thoughts!

If we begin our day by thinking about an
idea such as: "I am thankful for the knowledge that all things work together for good,"
we set the tenor of our thinking for the day.
Then if something happens to change our
plans, we remind ourselves that all things
work together for good, we trust God, we
trust our lives and affairs to God. We are sustained all day long by the sure feeling that all
is well, that God loves us, that we are impor-

tant to God and to God's world.

If we have set up resistance in ourselves to any condition or circumstance, we can let go of this resistance. As we think about ourselves and our lives, we can see that in many instances the very thing we resisted the most has brought the greatest blessing to us. So let us say to the condition or circumstance that seems to bind us, "There is some blessing for me in this. I now accept the blessing."

If we have to deal with an inharmonious human relation of some sort, we can overcome our inner resentment or resistance to the situation by blessing everyone concerned, including ourselves. It helps us to remind ourselves over and over that God is present in us and in all persons and situations, and that God can be trusted to bring about that which is for the highest good and happiness of all concerned.

Affirmations of Truth are habit-forming. A habit is the result of something that is repeated again and again. It becomes second nature to us. We all admire persons of character and worth; we may look on them as set apart, as especially endowed by heaven. But actually character is largely determined by habits—habits of thought, habits of reaction, habits of living—that are practiced not intermittently but consistently until the wish becomes the reality, the ideal becomes the actuality, the actor becomes the role, the role becomes the life.

If we were the lead in a play, we would memorize our lines until we knew them perfectly, we would become the part through knowing the character we were portraying. Shakespeare said that life is a stage and we are all players on it. Sometimes when we do not feel loving, when we are filled with feelings of resentment or bitterness or unforgiveness, it may help us to act a little. Shakespeare also said to assume a virtue, if we have it not. It is better to act loving, even if we do not feel loving. When we choose the side of love, love wins out, for love is stronger than hate. When we decide to act like a child of God rather than like an unhappy, embittered child of darkness, light wins out, for light is stronger than darkness. You cannot act like a child of light, a child of love, a child of God without beginning to feel like one.

Oftentimes we feel miscast; we feel that no one really knows what we are like inside, that no one really understands us. This may be true, especially if we have formed the habit of negative thinking and acting, if we have allowed our feelings, moods, and emotions to govern us and our lives. How is anyone to know what we are really like? Others will know what we are really like when we make the effort to think, speak, and act in the way that makes us feel right and happy within ourselves. If the habit of wrong thinking is deep-rooted, it may take quite a bit of persistence and effort on our part to change; but we can change. We can change our inner thoughts by practicing every day, in little ways, the lines of our true role in life. We can practice saying good things to and about others; we can practice thinking of ourselves as children of God; we can practice affirming words like: *I am loving; I am understanding; I am free,* until we begin to feel their meaning in our minds and hearts.

We can practice being the kind of person we long to be. And practice always brings results. Like the musician, we find that we progress from practice into a finished performance. Where at first it seems awkward or difficult for us to change long-fixed habits of thought, speech, and action, our "repeat performance" begins to count, the new pattern begins to assert itself. It becomes easier for us to be the keeper of our moods; it becomes easier for us to let the Christ love shine through; it becomes easier to live joyfully, peacefully, happily with ourselves and others.

You Are Here by Divine Appointment

A friend said that she once went through a time of questioning and depression. On the surface, she seemed to have everything—a good husband, a lovely home, children who were grown and living their lives happily. But every day at about 4 p.m. a feeling of loneliness and depression seemed to sweep over her. She would ask herself, "Why am I here? What is my purpose in living?"

There comes a time in the lives of most of us when something in us is not satisfied with material things alone, when the goals we have sought, striven for, and sometimes achieved, no longer seem so important. We may ask ourselves, "Why am I here? What is my purpose in living?"

It is really a good sign when we come to such a place, when we have such feelings, for it is an indication that we are growing and that we are ready for greater spiritual understanding, for a clearer realization of the Truth of our being.

Have you ever thought of yourself as being here by divine appointment?

When we think of the word *appointment*, there are two meanings. One: an appointment or engagement or specified meeting with someone or something. The other: being appointed, having some office, or degree, or responsibility appointed to you, conferred upon you.

We are here, each of us, by divine appointment. Just why or how we were brought into the world at a certain hour, on a certain date, to certain parents is a mystery we do not yet understand. But I believe it is not by chance that we keep a divine appointment with life, with the environment we come into, with the people who are a part of our lives.

Jesus said: "*For this I was born, and for this I have come into the world, to bear witness to the truth"* (John 18:37).

We, too, came into the world to express God's life, to show forth God-qualities, to bear witness to the truth.

Wordsworth wrote:

Not in entire forgetfulness,
And not in utter nakedness,
But trailing clouds of glory do we come
From God, who is our home.

We come into the world by divine appointment, and I like to think that we come "trailing clouds of glory." Jesus said: *"The glory which thou hast given me I have given to them"* (John 17:22).

If we come by divine appointment to meet life in our own particular place, at our own particular time, so also we come as appointees. *You did not choose me, but I chose you and appointed you.*

We have been appointed to represent God and God's Truth, to be channels through which God's will and work are done.

Jesus said: *"And I assign to you, as my Father assigned to me, a kingdom"* (Luke 22:29).

Where or what is the kingdom that has

been appointed to us, that we are meant to reign over? The kingdom of heaven, of course. And where is the kingdom of heaven? To quote Jesus again: *The kingdom of God is in the midst of you.*

By divine appointment we are here; by divine appointment we fulfill our destiny as children of God.

When we take hold of this idea of being here by divine appointment, it has its effect on every area of our lives and thought. We do not wonder why we are here, we know that we are here by divine appointment. We do not wonder what our purpose is. We know that it is to show forth God, to spiritualize our thoughts and feelings, to practice the Christ principles in our daily living, to make the kingdom of heaven a reality in our consciousness and in our outer lives.

When we take the idea of being here by divine appointment into our thoughts, it changes our attitude toward the happenings in our lives; we view situations and circumstances in a new light.

Does some situation seem difficult? We are here by divine appointment, and the situation

is a divine appointment we are meeting. In
meeting the situation with faith, courage,
and wisdom, we prove once more the power of
God's Spirit in us; we prove once more that
nothing in the outer is greater than the power
of God within us. *He who is in you is greater
than he who is in the world* (I John 4:4).

Does some human relationship seem inharmonious, lacking love and understanding?
We are here by divine appointment. We are
part of this relationship to bring peace to the
situation, to express God's love, to behold the
Christ in others, to help others find the Christ
in themselves.

If we feel bothered by interruptions when
we are trying to complete some project—the
knock at the door, the telephone call, the children quarreling—we are there by divine appointment and we can look at interruptions
and distractions as divine appointments. We
can see them not as slowing us down but as
giving us opportunity to prove that we are
not bothered by little things, that we are
greater than petty annoyances. Looking at
interruptions as divine appointments can
help us to go back to our projects with new

enthusiasm and interest, perhaps with new impetus. We may find that the distraction has proved a blessing in that we are inspired with some new idea.

Are we disappointed in someone or something? Has a relationship turned sour; has someone betrayed our trust? This, too, can be a divine appointment. We are appointed to the challenging work of rising above personal feelings, to the challenging work of knowing that we are all-loving, all-forgiving because we have God's loving Spirit in us. We are here by divine appointment and we have been divinely appointed. Knowing this, we hold steady, we know that in and through the experiences of our lives a loving law of good is at work, drawing our own to us, revealing new paths of joy and happiness to us.

When we take time every day, if only for a moment or two, to go apart and pray, we are keeping a divine appointment. When we think of our prayer time as a divine appointment, we never think that we do not have time to pray, that other things come first. We keep our divine appointment with God in prayer, and our time of prayer becomes a time of joy, a time of inspiration, a time of infilling of God's Spirit. It becomes a time of talking to God and a time of listening. As we listen in prayer, we hear God saying, "I have chosen you. You are my beloved child in whom I am well pleased. I have appointed you a kingdom. Enter into the kingdom of joy, of health, of peace, of light, of plenty, of love."

You Can Help Another

"What can I do for you?" I found myself asking myself this question when it seemed that all my efforts to help someone who had turned to me seemed unavailing. I wondered if I actually was of any help to this person.

At first it seemed so easy, so simple. All this friend needed, I thought, was the right idea. All she needed was to be reminded of the truth, to be told that God loves her, that God is in charge. I knew I could help her by having faith in her and assuring her of my faith and prayers.

But time after time I listened as she poured out her feelings of unhappiness, of despair, of self-rejection, of bitterness over the past, of fear of what was ahead.

She always told me how she was trying to pray, to make affirmations of Truth, and she was trying, I knew. But I began to wonder about my part.

I realized that sometimes when we try to help another person we end up by making that person dependent on us. He does not necessarily get help from us, but he gets satisfaction from having someone listen to him without criticism, someone on whom to unload his pent-up feelings of fear, anxiety, unhappiness, frustration.

I realized, too, that there is always the possibility that we, in our own way, become dependent upon the person who turns to us again and again for help. We may unconsciously assume a parental role and feel responsible for him; we may even feel that he cannot get along without us.

I am sure that most persons have had someone in their experience whom they started out trying to help, only to come to the place where they realized that the other person really did not want their help, certainly did not want their advice. What was wanted

was someone to be a listening post, someone
to lend a sympathetic ear. There was a need
to be cheered and bolstered, temporarily.

How do we help another? What can we do
for another? Is a listening ear enough? Is
sympathy enough? Of some help perhaps, but
apparently not enough.

But if this is not enough, are we to try to be
less objective? Should we follow our tempta-
tion to give advice? If we do so, we should not
be discouraged when our advice is ignored, as
it usually will be. We should not be upset if
our attempts to point out a better way bring
tears and the reproach that "you just do not
understand!"

We know that to be critical of another, to
be impatient with him, cannot help him and
only adds to his misery.

So the question is, "What can I do for
you?"

And the answer must be that, as much as
we may try to help another, as much as we
may long to see him free from problems, we
cannot live his life for him, we cannot do for
him what he must do for himself.

What can I do for you?

What can I do for you is something beyond just listening to you, helpful as that may be from time to time. What I can do for you is to pray for you in the highest way that I know, that is, to behold the Christ in you. When I behold the Christ in you, I am beholding that which is innately good and wonderful in you. On a personal level I may see all kinds of things that need changing in you—in your way of thinking, in the way you relate to other persons, in the way you meet life. When I behold the Christ in you, I see nothing to change. I see the changeless Spirit. When I behold the Christ in you, I am never discouraged with you. How can I be discouraged with the Christ? When I behold the Christ in you I do not hear negation, I see the perfect One in you which is always seeking expression. When I behold the Christ in you, I know that you do not need my help or advice, for I know that you have that in you which is your own sure light and guide. I help you most by remembering this and by truly holding to my vision of the Christ in you.

It is easier just to dismiss another person as difficult, as negative, as self-centered than it is to behold the Christ in him. But it is a freeing experience to hold to this prayer of prayers for another: *I behold the Christ in you.* This is truly to love another person. This is the way I believe Jesus helped those who turned to Him. He said: *"By this all men will know that you are my disciples, if you have love for one another"* (John 13:35).

Perhaps those we are trying to help the most, the ones we are most concerned about, only need our love!

What can I do for you? I can love you with the Christ love. I can love you with a love that accepts you as you are, that loves you for what you are, for when I behold the Christ in you I have every reason to love you.

What can I do for you? I can behold the Christ in you. I can set you free from any bondage on my part, from any attempt on my part to change you. I can let God do His work in you.

What can I do for you? I can love you as God loves you. This is the greatest help I can offer you. This is my most effective prayer for you.

Pray for Others

When you pray for another, you give him the greatest gift you have to give. And the wonderful thing about praying for someone else is that you cannot pray for another without feeling the blessing and the good effect of your prayers for him in your own heart, mind, and life.

Are you praying for another's healing, prosperity, happiness, comfort, freedom, guidance? The following meditations can serve as guidelines for you:

For one who needs healing

You are created in the image and likeness of God. Life and health flow through every part of your being. Vital energy is in every cell. Order blesses every function of your body. The breath of God-life is the breath of your life.

Whenever I think about you, I see you as whole and perfect. I give thanks that appearances are not the truth in God's sight. I have faith that all things are possible with God. I know that you are a spiritual being, that your life is "hid with Christ in God," that in God you live and move and have your being. I know that God is healing you now.

For one who needs prosperity

Whatever your need, God is the source. I know that your supply is now at hand. I see you accepting your good. I see your affairs blessed to overflowing with all the good God has for you.

There is supply for you; there is work for you; there is a right place for you to live. As I pray for you, I see you as God sees you— prosperous, blessed, successful.

For one who needs happiness

I pray for you to be blessed in whatever way will mean happiness to you. I cannot know the desires of your heart, but I know that happiness and joy are God's will for you.

So I now affirm that God is coming forth into your life as pure joy, as radiant happiness. I give thanks that the events of your life are shaping themselves into ways that are for your good and blessing.

I give thanks that the love of God is within your heart, and that this love is mighty to attract your own to you. I see you expressing the love of God. I see you radiant with the love of God. I see you happy, free, glorious.

For one who needs comfort

There is within your heart a Holy Comforter. You are lifted out of sadness and sorrow and filled with new light and understanding. I see you filled with the peace that passes understanding. I see you strengthened and fortified in your will to go forward in life. I see you quickened in faith and renewed in mind and body.

I send you my love. I send you my prayers. I affirm the oneness, the unity of all life. I see you enfolded in the eternal life of God, sustained and comforted.

For one who needs freedom

You have a Spirit in you that is unfettered and unbound. This Spirit in you knows no limitations, is not bound by fear, by feelings of unworthiness, by destructive habits. I see you as free, as the perfect child of God.

All the longings of your soul find perfect fulfillment in God, the Spirit indwelling you. The past no longer haunts you. Your feelings no longer pursue you. You are free! The self of you that God created is your true self. It stands undefeated, undaunted.

For one who needs guidance

The Spirit of God is like a compass in your heart. I know that this Spirit continually points out the right direction to you. My prayer for you is that you may be receptive to the divine guidance that comes to you from within.

In any decision, God is with you, your light, your Way-Shower. In any need, He is at hand, your strength, your wisdom, your ability to act unhesitatingly, to move in the direction of your highest good.

As I pray for you, I give thanks that all things are working together for your good. I give thanks that there is a Spirit in you which is revealing to you, step by step, the way that is rewarding for you.

Meet Change with Courage and Optimism

We say of one person, admiringly, "He never changes!"

We say of another, perhaps despairingly, "If only he would change!"

What is the difference?

There are some persons who are unbending, unyielding, unwilling to change, who are set in their ways. Any new idea, any new way of doing something is looked on with suspicion and distrust.

There are others who perhaps would like to change, to be different, but they think it is too late to change. They tell themselves and others, "I've always been this way." I was with a friend once who was inclined to be upset and impatient over minor things. Her granddaughter said to her, "Grandma, you must be patient." The response was, "But you know I've never been patient!"

There are those who are happy with themselves and with their lives, who do not like to have accustomed patterns disrupted, who look upon change as an intruder. One man said that he might as well not go to church because the minister said the same thing every Sunday. He always talked about the need to change. This man said: "I don't want to change. I like my life the way it is. I'm perfectly happy for things to stay just the way they are."

Change comes from a Latin word meaning "to exchange." So change is not losing something but exchanging something, and usually exchanging for something better. I believe that we resist change because we fear the unknown, because we fear that we will lose something which has come to represent security and well-being to us.

To change means to make different, to transform, to give a different course or direction to. We may fear change, but all of us would like to see conditions change for the better; we would like to see a transformation take place that would make life richer, happier, more meaningful.

Change is a part of life. We accept this; we know that all things change. But when we are actually faced with a change, we may find ourselves fearful and resistant to the change.

Even change that we have prayed for may frighten us when we are actually faced with it. Perhaps we have longed for a different way of life; perhaps we have wished for a different kind of work; perhaps we have wished that we could change our surroundings. But something in us may back off when the change comes; we may feel that we are not ready for the change; we may wonder if we shall be able to meet the new challenge.

People go through all kinds of changes— change of jobs, a change of residence. Marriage is a change, divorce is a change, retirement is a change.

Paradoxically, in meeting change, what we need most is a changeless spirit. Outer changes do not make us fearful, do not disturb us, when we are centered in our faith in the underlying goodness of God at work in and through us and in and through all the affairs of our lives.

When we say of a person, admiringly, "He never changes," we do not mean that he never changes his mind; we do not mean that he never makes changes in his life. We mean that he remains constant in his attitude of faith and courage.

Again paradoxically, the more we change and grow spiritually, the more we attain inner stability, the more we are able to be poised and serene, confident, and fearless through all things.

Certainly, we live in a changing world— standards seem to be changing, viewpoints are changing, attitudes are changing. But we also live in a changeless world, God's world, the spiritual world.

Love never fails.

The goodness of God never fails.

Truth is changeless and eternal.

The qualities of love and forgiveness, joy and understanding—these are changeless qualities.

Our understanding of ourselves as spiritual

beings, living in a spiritual world, governed by spiritual ideas, keeps us inwardly stable and serene and enables us to live happily in the world, undismayed by outer changes. Our faith is anchored in God. The changeless Spirit of truth in us enables us to be flexible, resilient, open, and teachable.

We live fearlessly, we meet change with courage and optimism, for we know that the love of God sustains us and our world. We have faith to know that all things are working together for good, for us and for our dear ones.

You Can Start Over

You can start over! This is something we all want to believe, need to believe. And, deep down, it is something we instinctively believe. There is something in us that even in the darkest night looks to the morning.

But as much as we want to believe that we can start over, sometimes we listen to our own fears and doubts or we listen to the voices of cynicism and pessimism that would have us believe that it is no use trying.

Sometimes a person will say, "It is too late to start over. I'm too old." It is not too late if we refuse to think it is; we are not too old if we refuse to think we are. This is where the starting over begins—in our thoughts.

That it is never too late to start over, that no one is ever too old, has been proved over and over by people who have had the courage and the wisdom to reject such thoughts.

Life goes through many stages and phases. Conditions and circumstances constantly change. We may resist these changes and feel threatened because accustomed ways of life are no longer possible. We may feel that we do not want to start over; we want things the way they have been.

But, often surprisingly, after having been forced to meet some change, we come to the place where we can look back and actually be thankful for it. We may even wonder why we found it so hard to meet the change that has brought us new blessings in its wake.

To start over implies beginning again in a better way. We start over when we let go negative thoughts and feelings about ourselves, about others, about life.

You can start over. Never forget this. Is it the end of a marriage? You can be like the friend who said: "I have just gone through a divorce after thirty years of marriage. I could not accept the situation until I made up my mind to help myself, and then it began to happen. The Lord has blessed me beyond words. I have come through darkness into light." Another friend who felt she was at the end of her life and her marriage said that as she prayed for light, her prayers were answered. She said that her life and circumstances did not change but that God gave her an entirely new outlook and she is keeping on keeping on. She finds that she can let go feelings of frustration about persons and events that she can do nothing about, and just behold the Christ in them.

Sometimes a person finds himself going through a time of depression. This was the case of a friend who said that in a state of dejection and feeling of self-pity she decided to try to lift herself out of it by giving thanks for her blessings. She also prayed for understanding and a renewed spirit. She said that as she prayed, it was as though God said to her, "Be a doer, not a don'ter." She said that she thought about this and could see that she needed to be more positive in her thoughts and actions.

Sometimes a person will say, "If only I

could have found Truth sooner my life would have been different." Rather than regretting that you did not find Truth sooner, it is more important that you give your thoughts, your heart, your mind to living and expressing Truth now.

We can start over. Where do we begin? Right where we are. We are always at a point of beginning again.

"I will restore to you the years which the swarming locust has eaten" (Joel 2:25).

The old has passed away, behold, the new has come (II Cor. 5:17). The old becomes new in that we are able to look at the past in a new light. All that has gone before becomes part of our soul unfoldment. We can be grateful for all that we have learned and gained and we can know that we are not bound by the limitations and mistakes of the past. They are gone. We can let them go. We can start anew.

All of us have had times of starting over. We have all known others who have changed the direction of their lives from negative to positive, from death to life, from sickness to health, from poverty to success.

Begin again! The hope of the heart, the
dream of the soul. If ever we feel restless or
dissatisfied with ourselves and our lives, it is
probably because we are ready for a change.
We are ready to grow, we are ready to let go
old thoughts, old ways, to enter a new way of
life and thought.

We can start over, for we are spiritual beings, and the power, love, and strength of
God are mighty within us.

Say to yourself, "I can start over." Give
thanks now that God's Spirit in you gives
you the will, the wisdom, the power, and the
ability to do and be all that you long to do
and be.

Do you wish that your life could be different? Fear not! It can be. Do you want to be
healed, to be strong, vital, alive, healthy?
Fear not! You can be. Do you long to be
needed, to be successful in your work and in
your living? Fear not! You can be. Fear not!
You can start over!

Make the Best of It

"We'll just have to make the best of it."
How many times, about how many things,
have we said this? Sometimes we may have
said it with an air of resignation. Sometimes
we may have said it because there seemed
nothing else to do. Sometimes we may have
said it as a show of bravery so that others,
who might also be affected, would be encour-
aged despite setbacks or seeming loss or failure. But if we really think about what we are
saying when we say, "We'll just have to
make the best of it," we see that it is really an
affirmation of faith.

To make the best of a bad situation is to
find something of value in it. It is to be will-

ing to do what we can to set things right. It is to refuse to give in to discouragement or despair. It is to let the mistakes of the past go, to know that we are not bound to them. It is, in essence, to begin again.

Sometimes we are called on to make the best of some situation that is a traumatic one, one that calls for all the courage and strength and faith we possess. Sometimes we need to make the best of what is really a small matter, but one that, if we allow it to, can upset us and make us unhappy and impatient with ourselves and others.

The world is richer because of those persons who have made the best of some bad situation or experience. We are continually impressed by the remarkable efforts of all kinds of people in all kinds of situations, to carry on, to remake their lives.

H. Emilie Cady says that it came to her as a great revelation that her hands were God's hands, that all mankind's hands are God's hands. She says that she stretched out her hands and looked at them and thought, "These are God's hands!"

We make the best of it when we know that

God works through us, that our hands are God's hands through which God works, through which God gives.

Every prayer we make puts us in tune with God and helps us to realize our oneness with God's presence and power. Every positive thought is a way of making the best of it. Every time we refuse to give in to fear and negative thinking, we are making the best of it.

People have literally changed their lives by changing their thinking, by determining to make the best of it instead of bewailing their lot. Like the prodigal son, they came to themselves and remembered their divine heritage as children of God.

If you have something to meet that seems to be beyond you, take your stand in faith, make the best of it. Know that God's power in you is mighty and that through His power you can meet all things. It does not matter what the appearances are, God is in the situation, good is in the situation. Fear not, you can make the best of it, for God has made you for the best and has ordained only the best for you.

The Spirit of God in You

Within all persons, all things, moves the Spirit, which is God.

"Before Abraham was, I am" (John 8:58). Beyond speech, beyond thought, beyond sight is this living presence, this light that forever burns, this power that is life, that is God.

The mystery hidden for ages and generations ... Christ in you, the hope of glory (Col. 1:26, 27).

"I am the resurrection and the life" (John 11:25). Jesus spoke from the divine. He spoke the universal language that all understand.

"I and the Father are one" (John 10:30).

"The Father is in me and I am in the

Father" (John 10:38). This is the eternal unity. This is the eternal truth.

In the face of the eternal many of the things that trouble our days seem trivial and unimportant. We forget many of our experiences, but we remember always the Truth that we learn.

"Is not life more than food, and the body more than clothing?" (Matt. 6:25) Food and clothing and shelter are essential to us all, but the joy of living does not spring from these. The joy of living wells up within us as we are conscious of God in us, as we touch the divine in thought and feeling, as we see ourselves as children of God, as living souls forever and forever making our way toward the unfoldment of the perfect self.

We sit in a room surrounded by four walls, but Spirit in us feels no walls. We listen to a clock ticking, but Spirit in us knows no time. We celebrate a birthday, but Spirit in us knows no age. We suffer a sickness, but Spirit in us knows no pain.

There is not Spirit and us; there is in reality only Spirit. We have made a separation where there is no separation. We have created in our minds a God outside ourselves when all the time God is speaking to us from the depths of our own being. We have tried to become holy when already we are hallowed, when already we are created in the image and likeness of God. We have sought God in churches and found God there because there is nowhere that God is not; because wherever we are God is.

We have called on God to help us and thought that somehow from God's heavens God answered, not realizing how close the heavens are—as close as the cry of our souls before ever our lips have time to form the words of a prayer.

We have thought of a few persons as holy, when even the meanest one of the street is filled with the Spirit of God within.

God is in all and through all. When you feel the presence of God, all things seem to shout God's glory. It is as though you had recovered sight after blindness. Like the man that Jesus healed, you say: *Whereas I was blind, now I see.*

Whereas you have been anxious and worried about yourself and your affairs, now you feel great calmness and trust in the eternal God who is within you, who is within all. You can say, "This too will pass," not with a feeling of resignation to unhappiness but with a feeling of inner poise that comes when you know that Spirit is greater than experiences, that only Spirit is eternal and untouched by the things that from a human standpoint seem impossible to bear.

When you know that you are Spirit, you are not afraid, for you know that nothing can hurt or harm or destroy the indestructible Spirit in you.

You are not afraid of life or death, for you know that, come what may, the Spirit in you is unchanging, unending, unafraid.

God Created You as You

God created you as *you*, and God does not make mistakes. You are a divine creation. You are made in the image and likeness of God. Do you believe this? I think you do, in one part of you, at least, for all of us have an innate feeling of uniqueness, of being a special creation, though we may not acknowledge it, even to ourselves.

You may downgrade yourself, you may have a poor self-image because you are thinking in terms of what you are not, rather than in terms of what you are. You think that you are not as good as you might be. If you only realized how good you are!

You can increase your self-esteem and form

a new self-image through the day by day application and practice of Truth principles. What does this mean? It means to change the tenor of your thinking. It means to learn to accept yourself as a spiritual being, as an important part of God's creation, an important part of life.

Quit thinking of yourself as unworthy. Nothing could be further from the truth! God created you; God sees you as worthy. As God's child you deserve the best.

Quit thinking of yourself as inadequate, incapable. Nothing could be further from the truth! In your divine self, your God-created self, you have powers and abilities, talents, and potentials that you have not begun to express and use. God in you says, "Be the self that you were created to be. Express that which you have been created to express."

When you do not give up easily, when you do not hold back in fear, when you do not bury your talents, you like yourself, even though you may be far from achieving goals you may have set for yourself. When you know and feel within yourself that you are giving your best, doing your best, self-approval comes. Self-esteem and self-approval come not because of what someone else says to you or about you, as much as words of praise help and encourage you. They come from your inner feeling about yourself.

Quit thinking of yourself as unloved. Nothing could be further from the truth! God loves you with everlasting love, and God has given you a great capacity for love. You feel loved as you give expression to the love that is within your heart, and the more love you express the more loving are your relationships with others, the more joy you feel in life.

Quit thinking of yourself as hemmed in by sickness or lack. Nothing could be further from the truth! Sickness, lack, limitation of any kind have no power over you. You are one with divine life, the life that heals and restores, the life that energizes and renews. You are one with the substance of God which is never diminished, which always pours forth abundance into your life and affairs. You can be healthy, prosperous, successful, free.

Quit thinking of yourself as held back by

other people or as unfairly or unjustly treated. Nothing could be further from the truth! No one or no thing can limit or impede you. What is yours by divine right cannot be withheld from you. Your own place, your own special role in life, cannot be filled by anyone else. No one can hold you back when you realize that God in you always makes a way, that under God's divine law, order, harmony, and right conditions are established.

Quit thinking of yourself as unneeded, unimportant. Nothing could be further from the truth! As God's child you are needed and important in God's divine plan. You have something to give that only you can give, you have ways of serving that make you needed, you are an expression of God's light and love where you are.

Quit comparing yourself unfavorably with others. God created you as *you*. You really would not want to be anyone else if you could. Appreciate others, but appreciate yourself also. Appreciate all the wonderful powers and abilities with which you have been created, appreciate your inherent strength and overcoming power.

Believe in yourself. Think how you have grown through the experiences of your life; think of the understanding and insight you have gained. Believe in your ability to cope with difficulties. Know that God believes in you, that God's Spirit of courage and faith are within you.

Beloved, we are God's children now; it does not yet appear what we shall be, but we know that . . . we shall be like him (I John 3:2).

This is what you are to remember, that you are God's child now, and that you are growing, unfolding, learning, becoming more like the divine pattern that is in you.

God created you as *you*. It is up to you to be the best you that you can be!

Fear Not Insomnia

People suffer from insomnia for a variety of reasons, but whatever the reason, anyone who has experienced it longs to be free from it. He longs for the bliss of an uninterrupted, restful night's sleep.

Sometimes sleeplessness has physical causes. Sometimes it is caused by mental tension or worry. But in any case, the need is to be able to let go, to relax, to rest. Sleep is something we take for granted—unless we have difficulty sleeping! Then it becomes of prime concern.

Those who are familiar with prayer and affirmations and their positive effect on mind and body try very hard, as a rule, to overcome sleeplessness through this method. Perhaps they are not always successful because they do try very hard. When we can't sleep at night, we are usually in an especially alert an vigilant state of mind. Our affirming Truth in this state of mind can be done with so much intentness and intensity that we make ourselves wider awake than ever.

When we affirm words of Truth, we may not speak these words aloud, but even our unspoken words carry a tone. This may be the clue, the key. When we are restless and wakeful, let us speak to our minds and bodies in a soothing, quieting voice. We shouldn't say to ourselves, "Be still!" as a command. We should say to ourselves quietly, smoothingly, softly, "Relax. Relax. Let go. Let God take over. God is in charge. All is well." Repeating such words many times will help us to feel relaxed. It is better than counting sheep!

As we let ourselves think of relaxing and resting, it helps to close our eyes and feel ourselves drifting . . . drifting down a stream . . . floating on the current of God's love.

We can learn to relax and let go in every part of the body by deliberately and consciously saying to ourselves, "Relax." Then we should breathe deeply. "Let go." Breathe deeply. "God is in charge." Breathe deeply. "All is well." Breathe deeply.

Insomnia can become a habit. We begin waking at two o'clock in the morning and every night seems to follow a pattern. Any habit can be broken. Insomnia is no exception. The way to overcome a habit is through replacement. Replace the unwanted habit with a desirable one. Bondage to habit also comes when we accept it, when we talk about it, when we feel helpless because of it. Let us not say to ourselves or to anyone else, "I just can't sleep," or "I always wake up at two o'clock and stay awake till dawn." We are convincing ourselves more than anyone else that we have let sleeplessness get the better of us.

Long before bedtime, in fact, early morning is not too soon to start, we should begin replacing the habit of sleeplessness. This does not mean that we should start early in the day to think of sleeping at night. It does mean that we should start early in the day to establish in ourselves a feeling of trust and faith in God as the loving presence and power in our lives, a feeling of trust in God as the healing power in our bodies, a feeling of trust in God as the harmonizing power in our affairs, a feeling of trust in God as the supply of our every need. It means, too, that we do not wait till nighttime to let go and let God take over in our lives. We do not repress our fears. We look at them; we see them in their nothingness, and we release them.

We should not be discouraged or give up if we do not break the habit of sleeplessness in just one or even many tries.

When we have allowed our minds and bodies to go along with a negative pattern, it may take persistence and practice in prayer to make an about-face. But it can be done. We are meant to live healthy, happy, free lives, and a good night's rest is part of God's good plan for us. For as the Psalmist puts it so beautifully, *He gives to his beloved sleep* (Psalms 127:2). We are God's beloved!

Remember the Minutes
that Count

An hourglass measures time in terms of minutes. Most of us do not think of time in terms of minutes but of hours and days and months and years. But there is a sense in which we live only in minutes. When we look back over the years we remember only certain special minutes; all the rest are lost to memory.

I think of these minutes which we remember as minutes in eternity, the times when we break through the clouds of doubt and indecision, the times when we are aware of our true identity.

There was the minute in your life when you realized the actual meaning of the idea of

God, when you felt God's presence and knew God's love. There was the minute in your life when you had insight into a certain problem and knew an immediate solution. There was the minute in your life when you stood breathless before beauty and felt all the wonder and glory of life pulsing about you. There was the minute in your life when you felt such a welling up of understanding and appreciation of another person that never again were you able to be intolerant or unforgiving of him or her.

We can have more minutes that count in our lives by living each minute in a spirit of love and faith and understanding. The years will count for nothing, the thought of age will disappear; but our memory of momentous minutes will mount, our joy in living will increase, as we take the opportunity that each minute offers to express the Spirit of God.

About
The
Author

Martha Smock was editor of *DAILY WORD* for more than thirty years. In that time she helped and comforted millions of people through her writing and her work in Silent Unity.

A native of Kansas City, Missouri, Martha was born in 1913. From birth, Martha was a part of Unity—her mother sent a birth announcement to Myrtle Fillmore, unaware, of course, of the role that Martha would someday play in the Unity movement. Martha began attending Unity Sunday school at age two, was a student of Charles Fillmore, and joined the staff of Unity School of Christianity in her teenage years. She became editor of *DAILY WORD* in 1944.

The magazine was an important part of her life even before becoming editor. She once said, "I begin each day at home and at Unity with the *DAILY WORD*. Our children and our grandchildren were reared on it. By the end of the month, the copy on the kitchen table is covered with jam and toast crumbs!"

Martha, who was an ordained Unity minister, was a beloved member of the Unity School staff and a popular speaker at retreats and conferences. She also authored the best-selling Unity books *Meet It With Faith, Halfway Up the Mountain,* and *Listen, Beloved . . . .*

Martha made her transition on July 5, 1984.

180-F-8699-7M-9-86